OFF TO CHELSEA WITH DIARMUID

St John of God Carmona Services provides
a network of residential and day services in
south-east Dublin and north County Wicklow.
As part of this network, Kildarton House in
Glenageary, County Dublin, provides day-care
services to children with intellectual disabilities
and also offers support to their parents.

ALL ROYALTIES FROM THE SALE OF THIS BOOK
WILL GO TO KILDARTON HOUSE.

OFF TO CHELSEA WITH DIARMUID

NICKI MATTHEWS, JACKIE BALL,
VALERIE DUFFY, GEORGE DUNNINGTON
& CLAIRE PRIOR

FOREWORD BY DIARMUID GAVIN

TOWN
HOUSE
DUBLIN

First published in 2005 by

TownHouse, Dublin
THCH Ltd
Trinity House
Charleston Road
Ranelagh
Dublin 6
Ireland

www.townhouse.ie

© the authors, 2005

© Photographs, Jackie Ball,
John Cullen Lighting, George Dunnington,
Vanessa Fay, Peter John Fellows, 2005

© Illustrations, Jackie Ball, 2005

1 2 3 4 5 6 7 8 9 10

ISBN: 1-86059-246-5

Cover design by Sin É Design
Text design & Typeset by Sin É Design
Printed by Creative Print and Design (Wales), Ebbw Vale

CONTENTS

Behind the Scenes at RTÉ

Claire Prior

WE KNEW THAT it would be an interesting few months when the first caller came on air and told Diarmuid he was 'a brat' but that she loved him and wished him well in Chelsea. It was January, and Diarmuid Gavin was in studio with Marian Finucane to invite listeners to come and help him build his garden at the Chelsea Flower Show. It was the year after the infamous lollipops (and boundary disputes with Bunny Guinness) and interest in his next 'big adventure' was extremely high. We knew that what was on offer was a gardener's Mecca – fifteen listeners would get the opportunity to work on-site with Diarmuid at Chelsea and to see his garden from concept to completion.

His criteria were simple; he wanted people who were passionate about gardening and for whom the chance to work at Chelsea would mean everything. They should send a paragraph explaining why they would love to go to Chelsea. That request unleashed the imaginations of Ireland's gardening public. Some wrote a paragraph, some wrote epics, and many sent photos of their gardens. We received numerous 'Odes to Diarmuid' and one innovator, Anne Morley-Lawlor who reached the final stages of the competition but didn't quite get to Chelsea, sent her entry written in gold lettering on a garden spade. In all, over 1,000 people entered the competition.

For us, though, it wasn't just about the yearning to get to Chelsea, it was about the stories that came with those entries; stories of how gardens were an oasis for many harried commuters and busy stay-at-home mums and dads. Others told of how gardening provided solace after the death of a loved one. Then there were the frustrated amateur gardeners, who itched to leave their day jobs and get their fingers into the soil full-time. The youngest entrant was sixteen years old, while the eldest was almost eighty – it seems that gardening doesn't discriminate.

From over a thousand entries, Diarmuid picked just 120 to go through to the next stage of the competition – a day-long gardening seminar in February at the National Botanic Gardens in Glasnevin. We broadcast the first of several special programmes following the progress of the competition from the seminar. Diarmuid described his vision of the Chelsea garden, and Mary Reynolds, former Chelsea gold-medal winner, told tales of her Chelsea experience and how Prince Charles mistook her garden for his own. It was at the seminar too that the aspiring Chelsea gardeners first got to meet George Dunnington – the Yorkshire gardener who would become the 'foreman' for the fifteen who made it to Chelsea and who would also prove to be a source of endless gardening secrets.

The next stage was a project that had been close to Diarmuid's heart for a long time. Kildarton House in Glenageary is part of St John of God Carmona Services.

They provide day-care services for children with intellectual disabilities and offer support to their parents. Their garden was in need of a serious overhaul. Diarmuid had met 5-year-old Sophie who attends the service at Kildarton and her mum, Erica, and had promised to re-design the garden as a sensory garden for children. The forty-five Chelsea hopefuls who made it to this stage had just one weekend to help Diarmuid transform the garden from a suburban plot to a children's wonderland. It was an exhilarating process to observe. While I, microphone in hand, went from group to group to talk to the gardeners, around me the garden became unrecognisable. Beds were cleared, soil and trenches were dug. Painted wooden totem poles emerged from the ground and a magical cottage with its own picket fence was installed. Hundreds of plants, specially chosen for their scents and textures to stimulate the children's senses, were placed in the ground. On Monday morning, Marian broadcast live from the garden as the children of Kildarton House came back to see the new garden for the first time, and we heard stories from their parents about what Kildarton and the new garden space meant to them.

Many of the volunteer gardeners told us that this experience had been so important to them that, even if they didn't get to Chelsea, they would be happy to have been part of the building of a garden which would be a haven for children for many years to come.

Yet, deep down, everyone wanted to get to Chelsea. A week after the garden at Kildarton had been completed, I phoned the fifteen people that Diarmuid had selected to work with him at Chelsea. In the pages to come, it is clear how significant that chance was to all of them.

People often think of radio programmes as something ephemeral – of the moment. But sometimes radio can create something lasting. I hope the programmes we made about this Chelsea journey – in

Behind the
Scenes at RTÉ

the Botanic Gardens, in Kildarton House and finally in Diarmuid's garden at the Chelsea Flower Show – tell of the bonds that can be created through radio, through gardening, and when a group of passionate people come together.

Claire Prior
RTÉ Radio 1
November 2005

**Off to Chelsea
with Diarmuid**

Foreword

Diarmuid Gavin

IN 1995 I BROUGHT my first garden to the Chelsea Flower Show. It was the start of a wonderful experience for me, working in central London to produce a display that, for one week of every year, is the Mecca of the horticultural industry. The garden, inspired by a Yeats' poem and called To the Waters and the Wild, was both a trial and a joy. Having the opportunity to work in such a creative environment in London for the month of May confirmed to me the many possibilities in the world of horticulture.

The following year, I returned with the help of the same small group of friends and created a vibrant city garden. It wasn't the previous year's lazy Irish scene, rather a contemporary – or what I considered contemporary – display inspired by nightclubs and pop videos, using glass bricks, illuminated paving slabs and stainless steel. On reflection, it wasn't brilliant and indeed wasn't regarded as such by the authorities. But at that stage Chelsea was in my blood. It is an annual chance for gardeners and garden designers to create something special and to show off excellence in horticulture or design. I loved it. It's both a trial and an ego boost. It was always desperately hard to raise the funds to get across the water; that has never changed. But you do get a chance to develop ideas along with a host of other garden creators, build a garden to your highest standard, have your game raised by the excellence of planting and construction that surrounds you and, most of all, meet people – old friends and new ones.

Inevitably, in the middle of creating one of these gardens, I (along with most other exhibitors) ask myself why I do it. The despair and the sleepless nights are very real. But the joy of having done the best you can possibly do is the best reward and the feedback from the members of the RHS and the public, both good and bad, is rewarding. With our first entry there I was struck by the amount of support received from the Irish gardening public. Over the years, this has strengthened and Chelsea has definitely taken on an Irish flavour.

A few years ago, I thought it might be good to share some of the experience. We had our own professional team to build the gardens, but my idea was to let ordinary people, whether they be expert gardeners or not, feel what I felt. So I looked for volunteers. Finding people wasn't hard. Hundreds applied. With great difficulty, fifteen were selected to help build our lollipop garden. Under their own steam, they made their way to Chelsea, put themselves up and reported for duty in groups of three. They were fantastic. They came from all parts of Ireland, worked hard with our team and, at the end of their few days, went back home.

Off to Chelsea
with Diarmuid

In 2005 we repeated the project, this time with the help of the *Marian Finucane Show* on RTÉ Radio 1. That whole episode started with a very simple idea. I'd been talking to Marian on the programme one day in January about another project I was involved in and mentioned (as I think I'll be doing for the rest of my life) that I was looking for a Chelsea sponsor. I spoke to the show's producer, Claire Prior, afterwards. We talked about Chelsea and I explained the process that we'd undergone the previous year. This was to be the start of something very exciting. Claire jumped on the idea and, with the aid of a large group of people, from the National Botanic Gardens and the Office of Public Works, to Gary Graham from Bord Bia, she, Marian and the team created some magic. People sent in poems and cards and letters, telling us why they'd like to be part of our team.

One hundred and twenty of those who wrote in were invited to a seminar in the National Botanic Gardens in Glasnevin, where great friends such as Annette Dalton and Mary Reynolds gave inspiring talks. In April, forty-five of those who were at the seminar were invited to help build a sensory garden for the children of Kildarton House under the guiding hands of Barry Cotter, and finally we had our fifteen ready for Chelsea. They were wonderful to a person.

You can't describe the feeling of building a garden at Chelsea. You couldn't recreate the atmosphere. To be in the city of London with a single-minded purpose, trudging to and from home or hotel, continually exhausted but with a smile on your face, is a an extraordinary experience. To begin to know people who share your passions, to work with them, have the odd pint and, as a team, build something different, something a bit special, with all the stresses, the time limitations and competition involved, is unique. To be doing it as part of a team, where your team is one of many working on the same garden, is hard to explain to people. But I think the stories of Nicki Matthews, Jackie Ball, Valerie Duffy and George Dunnington manage it very well.

Diarmuid Gavin
November 2005

**Off to Chelsea
with Diarmuid**

Before There was a Garden

Nicki Matthews

Nicki Matthews trained as an architect at the Dublin Institute of Technology in the 1980s and has completed the Master of Urban and Building Conservation.

Nicki's interest in gardening stems from her childhood days, when her parents bought an early Victorian villa because of the garden and its setting, without having viewed the interior. She worked alongside her mother in the substantial garden of the family home, which contained many unusual plants. Her love of gardening has endured and she now maintains a modest suburban garden.

Through her work as a conservation architect and subsequently as Dublin City Council's conservation officer, Nicki has developed an avid interest in both contemporary and historical design of gardens.

WELL THERE I was, at the Bull Ring entrance to the Chelsea Flower Show on Monday, 9 May 2005, a somewhat late arrival due to a delayed flight from Dublin. Was it passion that had brought me here to Chelsea? I was very nervous of that word, as I suspected the other Chelsea volunteers would quickly find me out if I dared to echo this sentiment. As I waited to be collected in the early-morning sunshine, I enjoyed the activity and bustle around me and I wondered for the hundredth time what I could offer as my reason for coming to Chelsea if Marian Finucane asked me the dreaded question.

'Passion' was a word that had been referred to continuously throughout the selection process. I felt that I was passionate about many aspects of my life, for instance my 'real' work as an architect, my sailing, my husband, of course, but gardening just wasn't in the same category. So how could I justify being selected and admit to be willing to give up time and energy to Diarmuid Gavin's Chelsea show garden if I hadn't that 'passion'? Ultimately, I think it came down to a deep fascination with Diarmuid Gavin's design ability (from my limited knowledge of some of his earlier work) and I really wanted to get up close and to have a good look at how it all worked.

Off to Chelsea with Diarmuid

From the first day in February in the National Botanic Gardens in Glasnevin (the 'Bots' as it is affectionately known), it was apparent that Diarmuid drew heavily from the well of contemporary architectural design and, in particular, referenced the work of several leading architects who used concrete for its sculptural form. That was an immediate attraction for me. Also evident was the fact that Diarmuid as a gardener/designer was not afraid of pushing forward the boundaries to express, or interpret, a new language of garden design that was representative of his generation.

This was a battle that was familiar to me, as it is one that also raged in architecture in Ireland during the 1970s and 1980s when many buildings were built as pastiche due to lack of confidence in innovative design and construction. So I was very relieved when Diarmuid was at pains to say during the course of that first day that there were people for whom gardening was simply all about plants, and then there were the likes of me who were intrigued by the design. This was very reassuring because, in the first ten minutes in the canteen in the Bots, where the 120 who had been chosen gathered to have coffee and to get acquainted, I had begun to feel that I shouldn't be there, as everyone around me seemed to be discussing the courses they had done or were applying to do. They talked about gardens they were commissioned to maintain, and an extraordinary number mentioned the fact that they had left gainful employment to set up landscape-gardening businesses. It all made me feel distinctly uneasy and out of my depth – better to go now than to be utterly exposed. However, the day in the Bots persuaded me to do otherwise and served to hone my appetite for staying the course, especially when Diarmuid presented his concept for his show garden in Chelsea to us.

This was a defining and surreal moment for me, one I will remember vividly for a long time. When I saw Diarmuid's concept drawing for the garden projected onto the large lecture-hall screen, I was simply taken aback. The build-up of the presentation indicated his architectural preferences and the fascination he has for concrete forms. However, nothing prepared me for the choice of planting in the show garden. Diarmuid put up a wonderful image of rolling hills covered in a mist of blue lavender clumps, which are so characteristic of the landscape of Provence in France. The night before I had been thinking that I might be asked about what type of plants I was particularly interested in. Drawing on the limited experience of my modest semi-detached suburban garden, I had thought of the clumps of planted lavender in it and thought no, don't mention lavender, it's too old-fashioned and people associated it with little old ladies with floppy straw hats.

George Dunnington was to offer reassurance on the matter subsequently when he stated that plants have remained the same forever, and that it's only the innovative way that gardeners consider using them that has changed and has created the excitement.

So Diarmuid was planning to plant a lavender garden in Chelsea! Wow! At that moment I knew I really wanted to be there to help create his garden. For as long as I can remember, I have had this thing about lavender growing in this way, producing a mystical blue wash across undulating hills, entrapping a kinetic energy in the same way that spun bundles of golden hay suggest a rolling phenomenon in the Irish countryside. I don't know where this identification with lavender came from, as I have never been to Provence. This image of blue lavender fields has always been with me, along with the subliminal desire to plant a garden full of lavender. It has just always been there and I remember thinking, this is so weird, it is just meant to be!

For the second time during the Chelsea challenge, I was having a momentary worry and wobble as I sat outside the entrance to the Chelsea garden site on that first morning in early May. Thankfully, my knight in shining armour arrived with a rucksack on his back – it was Phil Conway from Mayo, a father who had decided to stay at home rearing his three sons during their formative years. We immediately hit it off. I don't know how we quite got into it, but somewhere between meeting Diarmuid Gavin and Claire Prior, the producer of the *Marian Finucane Show*, and by the time it took us to reach the garden site, we had managed to identify that I worked as a conservation architect and that Phil was going back home to set up a construction company and that a conservation project would be his first venture.

Before we knew it, we had arrived at the site, suitcases and all. Our initial reaction was simply to stop and stare, somewhat taken aback by the construction work in progress. I quickly took the opportunity to see if I recognised any of the people who were to be my colleagues for the week. I kind of knew the names, but I wasn't sure if I had matched them with the right people. Group One was to include two girls (myself and Catherine Kirwan, a solicitor from Cork) and three guys, Phil Conway, Gar O'Leary, a landscape gardener from Monkstown, and Barry Murphy (the youngest member of the team), who was studying landscape design. George Dunnington was to be our co-ordinator and manager. Then, like an old friend, I could see George in his royal-blue overalls making his way across to us with a slow, steady smile on his face, immediately making us feel at ease and in the right place. The lovely, soft, lilting Yorkshire accent tumbled out and the stories followed one after the other over the course of the next few days. George was particularly pleased with himself as he proudly declared that many of the volunteers who were coming to work on the garden had been in his selection from those who had worked on the gardens at Kildarton House, in Glenageary, where St John of God Carmona Services provides day-care facilities for intellectually disabled children and support to their parents. As part of the selection process, the competitors were invited to help Diarmuid Gavin build a sensory garden that he had designed for the children there.

George ran through the various teams that were coming. A week of setting up had already taken place on the site and a construction period of a further three weeks was envisaged to complete the garden. Our team was the first group out and, much to my relief, the guys outnumbered the girls, as it immediately seemed to me that the work was going to be of a navvying nature. My gardening skills were not going to be to the fore – thank goodness – unlike Val, whose planting skills had been recognised early on by George while she was working in the garden in Kildarton House (he told us that this was why she had been selected for the final week's work). I felt immediately comfortable, for this was a scene that I was well accustomed to dealing with. Once we had our hard hats and high-visibility jackets on, I was in the groove. On the face of it, the teams appeared to be quite carefully selected and successfully co-ordinated with a nice mixture of maturity, enthusiasm, brawn, practical skills and knowledge of gardening. Cathy and I were, of course, the brains and the beauty of the team, balanced well by our hard-working and dedicated companions, Gar, Phil and Barry.

Cathy is a solicitor from Cork, and I had worked with her on the garden of Kildarton House. It was the first time I had met the guys, because the shed project I had been working on had kept me fully occupied for most of that weekend. George acknowledged the work that Jackie Ball and I had teamed up to do on the shed in Kildarton House. He told us that it was our attitude and approach to the job that had got us into his final selection. The task had been to completely transform a basic timber shed into a rustic garden building as one of the focal points in the garden. Both Jackie and I thoroughly enjoyed the challenge and we had got to know each other quite well, so much so that we were both disappointed that we were not going to be working together once again in Chelsea. Jackie was due to arrive in Chelsea as part of the second team of Diarmuid's volunteers and I spent most of my evenings texting her madly about the events of the day and advising her on what to bring with her. I still have a laugh when I think of the pair of us trying to build the shed in Kildarton from the perspective drawing. I was used to having everything drawn out with exact measurements. I recall our surprise when we realised that the pile of wood we

Off to Chelsea
with Diarmuid

were looking at had to become something that resembled the artist's sketch. Jackie was fully confident that I would know how to work it out because I am an architect!

I was to hear these words uttered again on the first morning in Chelsea, this time from Phil, because the first job we had to undertake as a group was to construct the site hut, which had been delivered that morning. The only problem this time was that the hut was in kit form, comprising large plastic components like outsized Lego pieces. I thought to myself, here we go again – another shed for Diarmuid Gavin with no drawings – there's a touch of déjà vu about this! The incentive this time to complete the shed within the schedule was the threatening weather overhead and the lack of shelter for our stuff. After much huffing and puffing, due to the unfortunate position of a very large mature tree, the colourful plastic components were clipped into place and the shed was successfully erected.

We were all well pleased with our efforts, because we sensed we were been closely monitored by Penten Construction Ltd, the construction team contracted to carry out the site works for the garden. I guess we were a bit of a novelty. Not to mention the fact that we probably appeared ridiculous – a group of gardeners (I think the collective name should be an 'enthusiasm' of gardeners) in the middle of a hectic building site. As an architect, I feel pretty sure that if *I* was in charge of a site onto which I was asked to let loose an enthusiasm of gardeners, then I, too, would be anxious, nervous and concerned. On the other hand, we thought we were the bee's knees and the cat's pyjamas because we were the chosen few and nothing was going to dampen our spirits. Not even the weather, which had suddenly taken a turn for the worst. I couldn't believe it. I had checked the long-term forecast for London and dry weather had been promised. Unfortunately, because I had wanted to travel as light as possible, I had overlooked putting in

Before There
was a Garden

appropriate wet-weather gear. Keen to share my anxiety with my deserted husband in Dublin, I texted him a message that said 'forgot my pain boat'. Fortunately, he understands that predictive text is not my forte (something he realised to his cost when, on a rainy day in Cork some time ago, I texted him to say that I was 'in dreadful pain').

With the rain about to pour down on us, it was obvious to me once again who were the serious gardeners and who were the 'potterers' like me. The serious ones emerged from the recently erected hut in full gear, while I prayed that the jacket I had on would hold out until the shower had passed. Rain did not stop play; there was no nipping off and waiting for the shower to be over. Thankfully, that was the worst of it for our week, which was extremely fortunate because I suspect things would have got exceedingly 'mucky' and a bit like the battlefields of the Somme if rain had continued *ad nauseum*.

Off to Chelsea with Diarmuid

At this point, the site consisted of a rectangular area of 9m x 23m, with a backdrop of mature trees. It fronted the main avenue facing towards the show area, which would be held in the Great Pavilion. The show gardens were laid out in pairs, each sharing a common boundary on a grid perpendicular to the main avenue. The gardens were surrounded by metal pathways to protect the routes and to allow access along one side of each site. To the rear of our rectangular plot was a large ship's container – like what you see on the back of a freight lorry. A good, big, rusty one like an old, battered metal bucket! I was puzzled to see this abandoned on the site with lots of timber framing surrounding it. The concealment of this large object was one of our key goals for the week. It was explained that the high part of the site was to be formed on top of this metal container, which was eventually to be fitted out as the hospitality room for visitors to the garden. The other role of this container space (which will eventually form the entrance to an underground car park when the garden is moved to

Dublin) was to create the effect of coming from underground up into a garden space – one of the key ideas behind Diarmuid's design.

Another task to be completed was the blockwork for the perimeter walls. This was already partially in place, but the main shared boundary had also to be clad with polished granite. Diarmuid Gavin's garden site was partnered in this show by Sir Terence Conran's garden, the designer of Habitat fame. We were all relieved to hear that issues regarding the shared boundary had been successfully negotiated and that relations were good, so much so that the vying designers had enjoyed lunch together. However, the work crew had all been warned to keep our focus within our own site and not to be fraternising with other competitors. We initially tried to follow this instruction, but we soon realised that talking and asking questions of fellow labourers wasn't an issue and Gar, probably the most experienced gardener in our group, found that information was freely offered and readily given.

Our first day was very much about getting re-acquainted with each other, and with George, and working out what the game plan was to be. We caught up on what the programme was, our goals for the week, and worked out where to get coffee, where the toilets were and, in general, how to survive. It also was apparent that there was great ongoing activity with the construction team, Penten Construction Ltd. One of the first surprises for me was the discovery of how a Chelsea garden is built. I had expected landscape gardeners. Instead, we had a regular construction crew, who seemed to specialise in domestic work, and this was their first time to work on a garden in Chelsea. From my perspective, I found an interesting difference in how builders approached the 'making of a garden' and how garden designers go about it. The level of information that a garden designer required to set out a garden intrigued me. It seemed to be more focused on the use

Before There
was a Garden

of 3D images and on an experienced eye rather than the exact setting out of measurements. This was a complete revelation to me. Of course I should have realised this on the day in the Bots when I was asked to make the presentation for our group and was mortified when I got an awful jeering for having produced a section through the length of my garden design. 'Too much information!' was shouted at me from the back of the auditorium. However, I was vindicated at the end of the day when Marian Finucane remarked favourably on my section drawing. She understood where I was coming from. That's the way architects are trained, to think and to design, and basically you get sued if things end up in the wrong places! Gardening was proving to be a very liberating experience – lots of creativity and no painful details or measured drawings.

It was apparent that I wasn't the only one struggling with the lack of 'working drawings' as architects call them. The construction crew found it difficult also. Penten Construction Ltd had a very international flavour to it; I had forgotten just how many Kiwis and Aussies honed their construction skills in London whilst exploring Europe. Matt was from Australia and he was a meticulous measurer and leveller. I expressed an enthusiasm for this activity early on and I must say I enjoyed this aspect of the site, as these were skills that had become rusty as I had become a 'pen-pusher' in more recent times. Creating convincing levels within this tight site in accordance to Diarmuid's design concept was, to my mind, a serious challenge. Even with my background, it was very difficult at times to get a feel for how it was all going to come together, especially as the clay was removed and brought back and forth from one end of the site to the other several times. However, fuelled on optimism and enthusiasm, we all kept the faith. We shovelled on cheerfully, we measured and checked, and then waited to see what would happen next. Sometimes things would reach such a level of

Off to Chelsea with Diarmuid

intensity with the mechanical diggers swinging to and fro that we could not remain on the site. That really wasn't a problem, as there was always something to be picked up or tidied up, and George always had a story to tell. This is how these extraordinary days of furious activity flew past. Invariably, we were on the site until late in the evening, as none of us were anxious to leave the job in hand.

The nature of the clay on our site was not particularly appealing as it was quite yellow, terribly sticky and, once walked upon, seemed to set like rock very quickly. However, the aspect that really attracted me was the content and variety of artefacts to be found in the clay. Sometimes I found small bones. That always gives you a fright on a site, but this stuff had been in and out of the site so many times that it probably could have told its own story. Then there were traces of previous show gardens, possibly dating back several decades judging by the old lime mortars and the roughish bricks that we found. The best find, though, were the large oyster shells, which really brought the context of the site home to me. The site was located close to the Thames and these shells showed how oysters probably enjoyed great prominence as a local food source in earlier times. The discovery of these shells echoed the research I had done into the development of Merrion Square in Dublin. I had been told by owners of properties on the north side of the square that seashells would appear in the gardens because, at one time, the sea used to come right up to the mews' lane at the rear of the properties. Indeed, the whole context of this site and its relationship to the history of the river and the development of the city of London was really spelt out as we walked along its banks. As we passed the church associated with Thomas More, I could imagine him being ferried up and down the river to visit King Henry VIII on court business.

Before There
was a Garden

At home, working on private projects and, in particular, on specialist reports, it is very easy for an architect to get distracted by the phone or the radio or indeed the conversation of others. Gardeners, on the other hand, seem to thrive on a steady flow of information and a cross-fertilisation of ideas and approaches as they work and at times the punchlines of stories provided a much-needed break. The endless flow of stories from George while we shovelled clay in all directions probably constituted the most informative times on the site with regard to real gardening. The work in hand wasn't real gardening, but more of a gardening challenge or an exhibition. In fact, because we were the first team out, I suspect that we were all a bit frustrated that we weren't getting our hands on plants or physically doing any planting. Instead, we had to content ourselves with the overview and the formation of the stage set which would be transformed by our colleagues over the subsequent weeks.

Off to Chelsea with Diarmuid

George had a wide and interesting repertoire of stories, both from his working life and his subsequent retirement (which, much to his amusement, had projected him into TV stardom). I remember two things in particular that he told us, which probably give a good insight into the character of the man. When we met up with him on the first day, George went out of his way to settle us in. He was very enthusiastic about the hotel that we were all staying in, mainly because of the buffet breakfast that was to be enjoyed each morning. In his opinion, it merited serious attention and sufficient time had to be allowed to do justice to the array of food.

George also told us that he had worked for an electrical power company in charge of a landscaping crew and that he had planned their work. Many of the stories he recounted had a resonance for me as I, too, had worked as a consultant (in my case with the Irish Electricity Supply Board). My role as one of the architects who would be called out to make recommendations on the maintenance of stations brought me to all parts of Ireland. Frequently, the issue focused on planting or screening, or the lack of it, for these industrial installations. George seemed to have fought similar battles in terms of trying to maintain planting at stations and to protect them from oil spills or chemical damage, not to mention vandalism. His job seemed to have focused and honed his gardening expertise and you could only imagine the difference having such dedication and passion must have made to the job. In contrast, Irish power/sub stations depended on contract landscapers who were asked to turn up only when there was a problem, rather than working as a proactive in-house gardening team who systematically plan and work their way around sites.

George told us that he once came upon a situation where the use of chemical weedkiller had been applied so liberally over a length of time that the run-off had damaged a forest of trees adjacent to the site. This story highlights the lack of understanding that people sometimes have about the appropriate use of chemicals in gardening (the analogy of using a mallet to crack a nut springs to mind) and it also illustrates George's views on when to avoid the hard stuff and when to revert to using more environmentally friendly products for the treatment of pests or for weed control – such as boiling up rhubarb to create a liquor to kill off dock leaves! In fact, both George and Diarmuid seemed to focus on the sustainability of gardening. Forcing plants to flower artificially early or prematurely was not favoured as a policy by either of them.

This seemed perfectly reasonable to me. Having a cold garden situated on top of a plateau in County Kildare, my experience is that a plant in my garden tends to bloom about a month later than the same plant would in a garden in Dun Laoghaire. Summer seemed to be late everywhere in Europe this year and I was certainly surprised that London wasn't dramatically warmer at

Before There was a Garden

this time of the year. As hot weather was now required to mature the ordered pots of lavender, we were particularly conscious of sporadic reports coming back from Europe. We were all keen to hear the updates on the progress of the plants in Spain and France and whether they would bloom in time for the final week of the show. We all wanted the blue, scented lavender flowers to be out. However, with regard to this one pertinent detail, Diarmuid's experience in such matters led him to state clearly in his design submission that the lavender might or might not be in bloom for the show.

Between stories, we had a more serious distraction in the form of a rather large and imposing site foreman called Mick, who was originally from Limerick. Indeed, Mick was not the only construction worker of Irish extraction – there were several 'brickies' originally from Ballyfermot in Dublin. On the first day, Mick circled our group on several occasions and we were aware of a number of remarks being made in passing, but we weren't too sure if they were insulting or helpful. As the days passed, our confidence grew and we (the girls) returned rallies with Mick with ever increasing effect. So much so that one day when he was mincing through the site with a very heavy saw, I told him laughingly that he was carrying the saw like a handbag! At once I regretted my humorous observation as I sensed that I might have gone too far by slagging this huge man's masculinity as he effortlessly carried a heavy piece of equipment.

I awaited my fate at Mick's hands and I didn't have to wait too long. We had all put in a good day's work and it was getting towards late afternoon and knocking-off time. The construction team, comprising the project manager, Ranjith, Mick and Matt, along with George and Hester (Diarmuid's representative on site), were up on the newly formed clay-covered bank at the end of the site. The height of the bank provided a great vantage point from which to view the other show gardens. We were working away on the lower section of the garden, keeping a watchful eye on the group on the bank as they planned the next move. I happened to look up and caught Mick's eye for a moment, providing him with the opportunity to finish me off. I heard the big voice with the Limerick accent shouting down to me, 'Well, you're not doing much with that shovel, are you?' What could I do but acknowledge the fact that I had been leaning on my shovel and reply, 'Sure Mick, I had to stop shovelling as I was so taken up with admiring you up there on the bank.' And that was that, we had reached an understanding, or least a happy truce.

With the construction and covering-in of the bank, we felt that real progress had been made on our watch, but we were still impatient to push on and I think we all felt disappointed at the thought of having to leave it in mid-stream. The garden was still looking like a building site rather than a sanctuary of peace and tranquillity. The cladding of the polished granite to the concrete block wall was progressing well and we very much admired the reflective quality and sharpness of the finish, especially as the white roundness of the pods radiated back into the garden. We could only imagine how well the colour and movement of the planting would also work. To compliment the black and highly polished surface of the shared boundary wall, a lower, plaster wall was in the process of being constructed, which would be painted an aubergine colour.

At least now there was talk of the plants arriving. Soil had been prepared and a final number of plants for ordering had been agreed on. We were told that the plants would be arriving from France and Spain in the next few days and that they would be packed on trolleys and refrigerated during transportation. The number and size of the lavender plants to be used in the installation of the garden was astonishing: approximately 800 in total. They were going to be planted and offset against ninety box hedges clipped into substantial spheres. A mixture of more 'loose or less formal planting' was to be positioned around the base of each pod, reflecting the function that each pod would have within the garden; for example, one was a potting shed, another an office, while yet another was a relaxing contemplative space.

The mornings for us usually started slowly, which was just as well, as we tended to work late in the evenings and stiffness was certainly a factor for me until I found the pace again. Also, although the weather was dry, it was a bit cool and our site was overshadowed by the large, mature trees to the rear of the site. I am not sure if it was excessive pollen or the building dust in the air, but we became aware of the number of people coughing and sniffling during the week. 'The Chelsea Cough' was a known phenomenon of site labourers/gardeners during the set-up weeks, and a few of us were starting to succumb to its effects. The work at times was a bit sporadic and, due to its heavy nature, small diggers were used instead of our manual labour. The jobs at times were quite labour-intensive. Lots of lifting of blocks, scaffolding, planks, shovelling of clay, more block moving, mixing up mortar, carrying in granite slabs and carrying out stones. It was all quite exhausting. The physical activity, coupled with being out in the open air all day and then the walk home in the evenings along the embankment to Chelsea Harbour, emptied the battery. So much so that to go out to eat in the evening took a super-human effort and sleeping in a strange bed posed absolutely no problem. Poor Barry had got a dispensation from his end-of-year exams in his college course so that he could work on Diarmuid's garden. God help him, he sat down each evening and religiously worked through his study notes to prepare for the exams that awaited his return. We looked at his notes with interest on occasion as they contained information of a very useful nature.

The highlight of each day varied tremendously. I remember being ecstatic when they hung the door on the ladies' toilet, replacing a very large curtain which

Off to Chelsea
with Diarmuid

one had no control over when one had to use the toilet. The bacon, sausage and fried-egg 'sangers' in the site canteen were a novelty that quickly faded. Another day, I had to make my way up to the King's Road through the Chelsea Hospital grounds. Dressed in my high-visibility vest, site boots and hard hat, I was a pretty incongruous sight amongst the gorgeously dressed shoppers in this very glamorous retail road. I had to buy sandwiches for a few of my co-workers who could no longer take the canteen food on-site and I also had to meet a cousin of my husband's who was living in London. I don't believe that I could have looked worse for such a rendezvous, covered from head to toe in a thick layer of dust, but my in-law was ever-charming and unmoved by the sight of me and actually suggested that we should go to a well-heeled joint nearby for lunch. Looking like an Irish navvy was not my idea of appropriate attire for Sloane Square or the King's Road, and I quickly declined in favour of a more humble eating place, where I could easily fade into the background.

The arrival of Diarmuid's pods was probably the most important event of our week. The circuitous system of delivering materials to the site meant that everybody who was building a garden at the time saw their arrival as they made their way around the show grounds on the back of the delivery truck. They reminded me of very large ostrich eggs and they seemed to bring out strong maternal instincts in all of us as we worried and fretted over their installation and their ultimate survival on this chaotic site. We waited with bated breath as they were lifted by a specially fitted stainless-steel hoop and gently dropped into place under the watchful and calculating eye of Hester. Once in place, we wrapped them in polythene sheeting but, inevitably, muck and water managed to get into the bottom of several of them and the job of cleaning them up was not without its drama. This task fell to Barry and Cathy. Barry, being the youngest member of our group, assumed the role of being told what to do. However, it was soon clear that he was not happy about adding more water to that already collected in the base of the pod, as the problem seemed to be getting bigger rather than smaller. Head down, rear end in the air, enthusiasm got the better of Cathy and, as she stretched into the pod, she broke Barry's grip on her jacket and ended up with a splash in possibly the muddiest puddle of water to be found on the site. Even Mick's jeers did not dampen Cathy's spirits and she emerged to continue and to complete the job with great dedication.

Cathy was probably one of the most genuinely enthusiastic and dynamic personalities I had met in a long time and I really enjoyed her energy. She was always the first on-site in the mornings and, with great deliberation, seemed to be able to move mountains. George had a real soft spot for her. Her attention to carrying out the most mundane tasks of shifting large stones, brick and debris entailed her carrying around a plastic bucket, like a designer handbag, constantly picking and sifting as she went.

The days were not only physically challenging but also mentally stimulating, as we were able to keep an eye on progress on other sites. In the off-periods or the lulls, we ventured off around the show ground and sometimes, on the way to coffee in the canteen, we would stop off for a chat on another site. Work on setting up the Great Pavilion for the specimen displays had only started, so the main focus was on the other show gardens of various sizes, styles and forms. The Australian team were rather exotic, as they were always co-ordinated in the same colour tops and shorts, a different colour for each day. We had endeavoured to do the 'teamy' thing by making a homemade T-shirt with a central lavender motif, surrounded by the fifteen names of the volunteer gardeners, as a memento of our collective effort. However, to his credit, Phil was the only one of us brave enough to show it off on the site. George was also given

Off to Chelsea
with Diarmuid

one to keep as a memento of the volunteers that turned up from all over Ireland for the Chelsea Challenge 2005.

Close to the Australian garden was the other Irish entrant on her first outing to Chelsea. It appeared to the inexperienced amongst us that Elma Fenton's garden showed real promise. One of the best aspects of the construction stage was to see the arrival of the raw materials at the sites and watch how these flights of fancy eventually came together. In the same way Diarmuid had conjured up a raised bank from a shipping container, Elma's team had glued and fibre-glazed sheets of marine-ply together to create a self-cleaning swimming pool, which was beautifully planted along the edge with water plants. The team working with Elma on her first garden in Chelsea happened to have been made up of the same people that had worked on Diarmuid's garden the year before, which may ultimately have been one of the vital ingredients that led to her doing so well in her first show in Chelsea. Phil was particularly attracted to the detail of the hedge, which was woven of hazel and had an unusual forked top.

Before There was a Garden

In fact, so intrigued were we with all that could be seen that we asked George, whenever a lull came, to spend some time walking and talking us through what other competitors were doing. As a result, we all ended up with many photographs of details that interested us, and purchasing another disposal camera was a common activity. This was a rather nice way to finish our week off, as most of the show gardens had progressed quite well and the basic structure and some initial planting could be seen. All of the large show gardens had features that commended them: the exquisite planting of the Laurent–Perrier garden with its hornbeam arboretum; the sumptuous Portland stone fence of the Sheik's Memorial garden, which contained a very chic plate-glass shelter. The traditional was well represented too by the thatched inn of the Chelsea Pensioner garden with its pond setting. Great energy was expended early on in the construction of the thatched structure, which had a scalloped roofline and rendered walls.

The contemporary designs of Andy Sturgeon and Terence Conran contained a certain 'wow' factor, which kept us watching every inch of progress. Andy Sturgeon, sponsored by the show's main sponsor, Merrill Lynch, created a workplace that was described in his brochure as 'an extension of the home which doubles up as a private garden in the evenings and at the weekends.' This garden had a particular resonance for me as a home-based worker and I fell in love with the falling sheet of water and dramatic pool setting.

Off to Chelsea with Diarmuid

Terence Conran's Peace garden was next door to Diarmuid Gavin's, so continuous observation of it was much easier. The key attraction for me of Conran's garden was, I suppose, the quality of the detail and the crafting of the oak-lined pool, which had water cascading from a sculptural stone wall at the rear of the site into a plunge pool at the front. It was also a very contemporary design, but planted in an old-fashioned style, featuring a specially commissioned 'peace rose'. An immediately obvious contrast to Diarmuid's garden was the fact that there were endless drawings and details of how to assemble and construct the garden. The only problem was that Terence Conran had appointed a team of landscape gardeners to produce his garden and, as we now know, gardeners don't like a lot of drawings and found the extensive information very off-putting.

The enormity and the reality of the task of building a show garden in Chelsea was really brought home to us on occasion. Hester was a constant presence on the site and watched every stage of the work as it unfolded. It seemed to us that there was a lot of building work associated with the creation of Diarmuid's garden, but the timing allocated to completing it seemed to be sufficient, so long as no great snags were encountered and the work kept going at a good pace. The schedule for completion of Diarmuid's garden allowed for approximately four weeks. It was to be finished, judged and viewed by the press on the Monday of the last week in May, the week the show opened. The following Tuesday was the day that the Royal Horticultural Society members had visiting rights to view the gardens. On the Wednesday of the same week, the public was allowed to attend and soak up the creativity of the designers. This year, the show was to be extended by one day, so it would be open until the Saturday. In reality, the whole event, which took almost one month to set up, was viewed by enthusiastic gardeners for a few days before being completely removed in the weeks after the show's closure.

This was an astonishing and awesome effort to put into a project that had such a short duration, especially when you considered the months of preparation and fundraising that the design team went through in the initial stages. Not to mention the fact that the design submission for the 2005 show was made a month after the previous show in 2004. I remember Betty, whom we met in Kildarton House, expressing the view that there was something really weird about creating a garden in a very short time. It felt even weirder to create a garden and to dismantle it before it had bloomed and reached its full potential. However, that was to be the way of it!

Before There was a Garden

There was to be closure in the case of Diarmuid's garden, as he had managed not only to get sponsorship, but also to sell the concept of his garden to an Irish property developer. The garden was to be incorporated into a new residential scheme in the Docklands on Hanover Quay in Dublin. This meant that the garden would have a life after the Chelsea Show and Diarmuid was already working on how to modify it, making a more maintenance-free design for a communal garden by specifying clumps of long grasses instead of the original lavender plants.

And so our working week came to an end all too quickly. The bags were packed and left ready for the dash to the airport. On our last day, we were anxious to put in a good day's work, but had decided that it would be easier if we were all to leave together late in the afternoon. Everyone agreed to this except Barry, who was having real difficulty tearing himself away from the project and, as he was booked on the last flight out of London that evening, we finally left him behind in the thick of it.

We said our goodbyes and had our photograph taken with George. There was definitely a subdued air about us all. Then it really was time to get moving to catch trains, planes and automobiles in all directions. As we were about to leave, Mick, the mighty foreman, was in the middle of the site swinging the mini-digger around, moving clay towards the front of the site at a fair pace. There was no way to approach him to say goodbye. There was only one thing to be done. With a loud shout, I waved over to him, bidding him *adieu* and blowing him a big kiss with a wave of my arm. The unprecedented gesture caught him off-guard and, to my satisfaction, we had one more laugh at each other – it was a fitting end to my part in the first stage of the project.

Off to Chelsea with Diarmuid

Travelling back home and *being* back was very difficult for a few days. There was a lot of catching up to do, workwise, but there was also considerable distraction and exhaustion associated with the week we had spent labouring on the site. The photographs of our week's work were circulated by email the minute they were downloaded from the camera so that the next team, and the final team after that, would have some feeling for what they were heading into. Health warnings were issued and raincoats and teabags were recommended to sustain the soul. Progress reports came back by text and the completion date grew steadily closer. Before we knew it, we were packing once again to reunite in Chelsea and to visit the finished garden – compliments of the *Marian Finucane Show*, who were going to broadcast from the finished site. We were going to see first-hand whether or not our colleagues who had followed us to Chelsea had managed to deliver the same high standard of workmanship that we, the first team, had established as a precedent!

**Before There
was a Garden**

Provence comes to Chelsea

Jackie Ball

Jackie Ball studied visual communications in the College of Marketing & Design and subsequently ran her own design consultancy for twelve years.

She married Edmund in 1987 and they moved into their first home, which had two small patches of grass instead of a garden. Jackie found the perfect book, *The Small Garden* by John Brookes, and caught the gardening bug (she ended up putting a garden on the roof!)

She now divides her time between her work in ceramics and her work with children through the Artist in Schools scheme. She has designed gardens for family and friends, while she describes her own garden as very much a work-in-progress.

Jackie lives with Edmund and their two children, Sarah-Louise and Mollie, in Sandycove.

JUST FINISHED WORK on the garden of Kildarton House – what a great weekend! Volunteering to go in at 7 a.m. on Monday, 11 April had seemed like a great idea on the Sunday night. It didn't seem so great when the alarm went off and all my joints had seized up and were protesting painfully as I tried to get out of bed. But I did make it and it was a great idea, for I got to see the garden. I hadn't seen it properly the previous night, as Nicki Matthews and I were still finishing the shed at close of work. I also got to see the children arriving – the look of excitement, wonder and disbelief on their faces. This was definitely not the garden they had left behind the previous week.

The Marian Finucane Show was broadcast live on that same Monday morning. Marian spoke to a few of us, and I would have liked to be witty, intelligent and funny when I heard her saying '*Cá bhfuil* Jackie?' I was none of these things, but I did manage to answer her questions, even though the one about the back-to-front shed threw me. I discovered after the interview that there was a rumour (malicious!) that we had put parts of the shed up back to front. We hadn't. In fact, the shed was actually out-side-in. We had spent a good part of the weekend completely encasing a common-or-garden garden shed in cedar decking.

Everyone who had turned up that morning was delighted with the final result and the general feeling was that if they didn't get to Chelsea it wouldn't matter, as this had been such a great experience. I kept quiet on this one. Although I completely agreed about the experience of working on the gardens of Kildarton House, it would matter to me not to get to the next stage. I had really set my heart on going to Chelsea.

It was a long, long week after that: waiting, more waiting and hoping.

Lunchtime on Monday, the mobile rang, 'Claire Prior here. Can you talk?' The moment had arrived. Eek! But yes, I could talk. And there it was: an invitation to Chelsea to work on Diarmuid Gavin's garden. Three groups, each consisting of five people had been selected. Each group would work for four days on Diarmuid's garden. More details would follow. My youngest daughter Mollie, who was off sick from school, jumped around the kitchen with me.

I hadn't told many people about my efforts to get to Chelsea, although some had heard me on the radio, discussing my expertise with power tools. I texted the good news to family and close friends, all of whom were delighted for me.

The following week, still on a high, I got my dates and the names of the other people in my group: Donal D'Arcy from Skerries, keen gardener and all-weather golfer; Mark Phelan from Kilkenny, chef; Gráinne Doyle from Enniskerry, mother of two; Kathleen Dorrian from Donegal, mother of two boys and keen gardener. We were going to be Group Two, working from Saturday, 14 May to Tuesday, 17 May.

The next two weeks were completely insane. I had three art classes a week to juggle, I had to produce artwork and film for a yearbook for my eldest daughter's school, and I had a ceramic wall panel to fire and finish as part of the Artist in Schools scheme with fourth class in the Harold School in Glasthule. I was looking forward to the break I was going to have in Chelsea!

The flights were booked – good old Ryanair. I travelled a day early to stay with my sister Nicola, another gardening fanatic, who lives in Liphook. We visited Wisley, as always, for coffee and a quick walk around the gardens. It was funny to look at their display gardens and think that in a few days I would be involved in working on something similar.

Nicki and Catherine from the first group had both texted me with good luck wishes and things I needed to know: what to bring, where to eat and a small amount of what to expect. On the train up to London on Friday, I thought and thought about what I was expecting to happen over the next few days.

When I arrived at the hotel, I checked in, found my room, unpacked, and texted Donal, whom I knew would be arriving at any minute. We met up for a drink in the bar, had something to eat and had an early night, as we were due in work at 8.30 a.m. the following morning.

The day had finally arrived. It was 8.00 a.m. and in half an hour the Chelsea dream would begin. Downstairs, breakfast had already started and, by the time I arrived, Gráinne and Kathleen were finishing up their full Irish and Donal and Mark were on coffee. I couldn't eat; it was too early and I was nervous and excited. In my bag I had a raincoat, two pairs of gloves, a hat, sun cream, plasters, a bottle of water, paper, pencil, camera…the kitchen sink.

'Chelsea Hospital, Bull Ring entrance please.' With these words to the taxi driver, we set off for our first day's work on the Chelsea Flower Show. Our instructions had been specific; someone would meet us with passes at the Bull Ring entrance at 8.30 a.m. on Saturday. So that was where we waited – on the bench on the roundabout in the middle of the road in front of the Bull Ring entrance.

Off to Chelsea with Diarmuid

This is the main vehicular entrance into Chelsea and it was already busy. There was a steady stream of lorries, trucks, vans, trailers and cars all queuing to enter. First, though, the drivers had to get past traffic security – clipboards, walkie-talkies and no messing. Identification is checked, radioed through and then the wait begins. When the all-clear is given, specific instructions are provided about where to go and how long they can stay there. While we were waiting, in between taking group shots of us all with the Chelsea sign in the background, we watched one articulated lorry in particular. It was very, very long and the arched entrance appeared to be dwarfed by it. Added to this, the angle for approach was awkward; a roundabout and bench (with us on it) were in the way. Despite all this, and an audience of five, the driver managed to successfully manoeuvre his way into the gardens. We gave him a well-deserved round of applause.

As well as the traffic security, there was regular security at the gate. It was a very interesting half hour as we waited for our passes. The traffic never stopped. Diarmuid's representative, Hester, eventually arrived to collect us; she had been delayed trying to round up the five extra passes needed to get us in. These passes were very precious and, on occasion, Hester explained, they would have to be borrowed back to get other people in.

At last I was in. I had entered the surreal world of the Chelsea Flower Show, an alternative reality inhabited by gardeners, designers, builders, labourers, security and, of course, the spiritual home of the Royal Horticultural Society.

George Dunnington, dressed in his customary blue overalls, was there to meet us with hugs all round. It was great to see him again, as he had been so lovely to work with at Kildarton House. Once all the introductions had been made, we were issued with high-visibility vests – to be worn on site at all times. Ranjith, the construction engineer from Penten Construction Ltd, gave us the health and safety talk over a cup of coffee. On George's lead, we took the long way back to the site, looking at the other gardens, which were all at various stages, some more complete than others.

Provence comes to Chelsea

Diarmuid's garden was most definitely *under construction*. The pods had blue plastic sheeting half draped over them for protection. At this stage, there were three levels: the bank at the back, the areas where the pods were resting, and two circular, sunken areas where brickwork was being laid as a bed for the paving. Brown and white were the predominant colours. Nevertheless, you could see the bones of the garden emerging and, in comparison to the other sites around us, it appeared much more interesting. The black polished-granite tiled wall running the length of the garden was simply stunning.

Back on site, our first job was to tidy up the area around us. Each garden had its own space for storing tools, machinery and plants. In our case, this space was to the front and side and ran the full length of the site. The builders were not always the tidiest and, as George is particular about his working environment, there was a lot of 'housekeeping' to be done. This entailed clearing all debris into skips, sweeping the paths and grass area and tidying away any unused blocks, wood and other leftover material into the builders' trailer or finding an alternative home for it. This took up a lot of our first morning.

Graham, the BBC cameraman who had trailed us in Kildarton, was back with us again. There were a lot of tough questions to answer, such as:

'What are you doing there, Jackie?'

'I'm raking.'

'Why are you doing that?'

'I'm doing George's housekeeping, tidying up.'

'Are you any good at it?'

'Improving all the time.'

It's very difficult to think of something clever and witty while you're raking rubble with a camera in your face, wearing gardening gear and a luminous vest – it's not going to be a great fashion moment either. My daughters, Sarah-Louise and Mollie, had told me in no uncertain terms before I left to make sure that 'I looked OK and that my hair wasn't in a state.' They would be quick to remind me of that and, sure enough, while I was back home watching the Chelsea highlights on the television later that month, I got a text from my Chelsea colleague Mark, saying 'should have brushed your hair!' Oh well, my three minutes of fame and it had to be a bad-hair day. That's life for you.

Diarmuid arrived that afternoon and he took us across to the canteen for a cup of coffee. This was on the far side of the gardens and getting there meant walking around the perimeter of the Great Pavilion. This is what we had done previously with George. Diarmuid though, went straight through the Great Pavilion. It transpired that he never looks at any of the other gardens while his

Off to Chelsea with Diarmuid

is being built, so he comes in to the garden show through the Bull Ring entrance, walks straight ahead into the Great Pavilion and comes out at the exit directly in front of his own garden, thereby avoiding everyone else's. This was always the way he came and went while we were there. We, on the other hand, were very interested in seeing the day-to-day progress of the other gardens, so it became our habit to take the direct route through the Great Pavilion for coffee breaks. Coming back, though, we always took the longer and more scenic route. After our first day, we didn't have breakfast (a movable feast that could happen anytime between 10 a.m. and 11 a.m.) until we got to the site.

Over coffee, Diarmuid produced the final artist's impression of the finished garden. This had changed slightly since our time at the Bots (the National Botanic Gardens in Glasnevin). The paths were no longer two circles, but had become two overlapping C's. This was the only drawing of the garden: there were no elevations, sections or plans and not a measurement in sight, and the only other person with a copy of the design was Hester. Diarmuid talked to us about the final garden design. Originally his intention was to fill the rolling hills of his garden with a single variety of grass, but somewhere between his sketch and instructions to the illustrator, all this changed and the grass had become a sea of lavender. It was a very brave move to limit his planting to just two varieties of plant: lavender and box. He was quite happy to answer any questions we had about his layout and design. Sitting there having a coffee and a chat, it really felt as if we were all very much part of his team. This was underlined by the fact that the layout we were looking at was a proof copy of the leaflet that would be handed out to the public when the gardens were open.

Our construction team were builders who were used to working with architect's drawings, where every detail is marked and measured from every angle. All they had

Provence
comes to
Chelsea

to go on for Diarmuid's job was this one illustration. This was a novelty for them, although not always of the amusing variety. Beside us, Terence Conran had employed landscape contractors and had provided them with the full architect's compliment of drawings. They were baffled. Normally, the landscape gardeners worked from an artist's impression or sketch. Both teams were looking longingly at each other's 'plans'. Luckily, there was a very good working relationship between them and help and advice were willingly exchanged.

Digging was to be a major part of our four days. We shifted tons of soil from one place to another, and sometimes we shifted it back again. It was hard to get those slopes right the first time, or even the second time. In fact, sometimes it took a third, fourth and fifth attempt. That day, we had our first real encounter with Chelsea soil.

Off to Chelsea with Diarmuid

Chelsea soil is made up of rubble, broken drainpipes, bits of concrete, stones, rocks, oyster shells (Chelsea pensioners living the good life?), sea shells, bricks (at least one intact), bones, more rubble and, if you're lucky, you might find some clay. This is a result of years and years of show gardens being built here and then demolished. Archaeologists could probably have a field day examining the detritus left behind over the last fifty years. Despite all this, Chelsea soil is very, very precious.

Ten days into construction and the ground had been well compacted by diggers, JCBs, builders and general traffic. Even breaking the soil was hard work. On the Saturday, we couldn't do too much as bricks were in the process of being laid as a base for the path. Any shovelling would interfere with this.

We ended Day One mixing cement to grout to secure the brick base. Departing the site at 6 p.m., we left behind a much tidier, more organised site than the one we had arrived to.

Donal, Mark and myself hailed a taxi on the King's Road and headed home, while Kathleen and Gráinne took the long way home via the shops. In the taxi, we agreed that we would taxi in and out every day. I was relieved at this, as I have a gammy knee and a dodgy ankle and foot, the result of being knocked down by a motorbike as a teenager. This comes back to haunt me on a regular basis and, in the normal run of events, I avoid excessive walking. Pleasure and walking don't really go together in my world. Too much one day usually means hobbling my way through the next and, although I didn't want to be the only one using a taxi, I would have had to do it to get through the next few days.

Back at the hotel, we retired straight to the bar – muck and all – for our daily *après*-dig pint. We had earned it! We had dinner later at a great pub that had been recommended by Nicki and then back to the hotel to crash for the night.

I woke up the next morning at about 5 a.m. and couldn't get back to sleep. Lying there trying to convince myself that I was sleepy didn't work, so I made myself a cup of tea and watched some truly awful early-morning TV. I caught the weather for the day and worked out what layers to wear: T-shirt, jumper, sleeveless jacket, fleece. My rain jacket was in the bag as usual. It was very cold in the mornings because our site was in the shade and the temperature fluctuated a lot depending on the level of digging activity.

Provence comes to Chelsea

Sunday was a lovely day, sunny and warm. A lot of the sites were quiet, some with no activity at all. We arrived bright and breezy at 8.30 a.m. Our day began with – guess what? – yes, shovelling. A load of soil was delivered that had to be put in wheelbarrows and distributed around the garden.

I have already mentioned the incredible level of security we had to pass to get in either on foot or by car. There were also members of the Royal Horticultural Society's own security staff. In general, they were older gentlemen in shorts who drove golf buggies at intervals around the gardens, clipboards and pens at the ready. One of these eagle-eyed officials spotted some illegal soil-dumping in a skip near our site. Probably because we were the amateurs, we were blamed and reprimanded severely for this. Actually, it was Hester who got the telling off. We protested our innocence and let it be known that it wasn't us. The culprits had been spotted by us, but had got away with it.

Another rule worth mentioning, and one which we thought was absolutely hilarious, was the speed limit. They actually have signs proclaiming '5 mph: walking speed limit'. Mark and myself had to keep a firm eye on Donal; he was known to exceed this limit on the odd occasion. I did break into a run once while chasing a trolley of lavender, but luckily Mark was on hand to correct this oversight. We learnt the correct pace from our leader and mentor, George. On one occasion, he had gone to meet a delivery at the gate. On offering to hop into the cab and show the driver where the garden was, he was told in no uncertain terms that the driver would follow him if he walked ahead. Off George went and, as he walked in front of the truck, he decided to show the driver 'the Chelsea walk'. He slowed his pace down to a slow-motion army walk: step, pause, mid-step and step again, and that's how he walked around the entire Chelsea perimeter, following the one-way system to the site, which was almost back to where they had started out. The truck shuddered in first gear all the way round.

The curved path was to be a major design feature in the garden. Marshalls were the company who had made the paving slabs to Diarmuid's specifications. Their crew arrived on the Sunday morning to install the paving. Around the back of the site, cluttering up our tea area, were the metal bases for the paving. This came in sections, each roughly three-foot high. To all intents and purposes, it was like a metal table frame. Each frame would support two or three of the paving slabs that we helped to carry to the centre of the garden where they were to be put in place. This whole process was a bit like a jigsaw puzzle, as each metal section had to be secured to its sister sections.

Off to Chelsea with Diarmuid

When this had been done, Hester supervised the positioning, referring to her plan, which at this stage had almost disintegrated from being pulled in and out of her pocket. The two semi-circles were twisted and manipulated into place and then bolted securely to the brick base. Sheets of marine ply, which had been cut to shape and numbered, were then fastened to the frames. Finally, the paving slabs were unpacked from their specially made wooden crates. This was our first proper glimpse of them. They were pink and made of highly polished cement. In the original design, they were to be white, rendered concrete, which would have been difficult to clean and maintain. The surface finish and colour, a light salmon pink, was great, although there was concern that anything tipping off the corners of the slabs would chip them immediately. In fact, a couple of them had already been chipped. Everyone stayed clear, leaving Marshalls to unload and carry each paving slab on site. None of us wanted to be responsible for any accidents, particularly as there were no spares! Each paving slab had been numbered on the back and, slowly but surely, they were brought down individually and laid in place. The idea was that the path would appear to float between the planting, which would add subtle colour to the whole scheme.

One man was in charge of the placement so, as you can imagine, it was quite a slow process: scrutinising each piece, deciding where it needed to go, placing it and moving on to the next piece. By the time we went for our coffee break, a lot of the path seemed to be in place but, by the time we came back, it was back to square one – or in this case, slab one.

As the paving slowly began to wind its way around the garden, we concentrated on clearing and tidying the areas around the garden. Ninety *buxus semperivens* (box-ball hedging) were due to arrive that afternoon. At last we'd get to see a plant!

Provence
comes to
Chelsea

As I mentioned, the paving had been packed in specially made crates. These were now dismantled and we carried them to the wood skip. The RHS had an area beside the general skip where discarded wood could be left. This was cleared on a regular basis and, I presume, recycled in some way. The wood we were dumping was good 3 ft x 1 ft deal – what a waste – and there was no way any of us could carry it home!

As it turned out, The Fetzer garden took the bulk of the wood on our recommendation and encouragement. The members of this crew were very friendly. Their garden was really lovely and was already at the planting stage. The focal point was a wonderful fairy-tale castle, made entirely from recycled wood that had been gathered at the Fetzer vineyards in California. It had been designed and built by a talented young Californian who very kindly gave us a guided tour of it. It was circular, tall and narrow with a turret-style roof. There was a small room with a few alcoves and benches at ground level. They had even thought of including special holders for wine bottles. Circling the outside was a wooden staircase, complete with banisters. The staircase led to a rose-clad balcony from where you could view the garden, which was planted with very pretty wildflowers, primarily in yellows. This garden was a lot smaller than Diarmuid's, close to half the size but, funnily enough, it still came under the same class for judging – the show-garden section.

The builders had finally agreed to remove some of the excess tools, wood and bricks from the site. Two of us were asked to give a hand unloading the van at the builders' depot, so off Gráinne and myself went. Unfortunately, it was a gloriously sunny Sunday in the centre of London and it seemed as if everyone in the capital had set off on day trips at the same time. It took us two hours to get there in the stifling heat, most of which we spent stuck in traffic. The unloading itself, when we finally did get to the depot, was mercifully brief.

I was beginning to wonder if the heat had affected my brain when it was announced that we had to collect some equipment at Ranjith's temple. But no, it wasn't heatstroke – Ranjith did own a temple. While trying to park there, the driver had a small run-in with a parked car, the only injured party being an indicator light. There was some kind of ceremony taking place at the temple and everyone was dressed in white. There were flowers, candles and fires everywhere. We were wearing our gardening gear – mucky boots and luminous high-visibility vests – so we felt quite self-conscious and out of place. We collected what we needed and didn't hang around. Our return journey was prolonged somewhat because we had to stop at a garage to buy cleaner to try to remove the ingrained skid marks running along the side of the van, a reminder of the collision.

When we eventually got back to the garden, the path was almost complete and it looked great. The box had arrived, all ninety pots of it. At last something green and alive in the midst of the muck. The box balls were over 2 feet in diameter, perfect green spheres, and much bigger than I had expected. The pots were bone dry and, as it was a hot day, a large drink of water was called for, so I nominated myself for the job. This helped me to calm down and recover from the frustration of the heat, the van and the endless traffic we'd just been through. My dread and panic at the thought of missing even a minute of the whole Chelsea experience faded away as I thoroughly watered each and every one of the plants.

As soon as the path was finished and Marshalls had cleared all their tools out of the way, George issued us all with shovels and spades. Back to shovelling. This time we were filling in the area underneath the paths to hide the concrete base, the feet of the metal frames, and a lot of rubble. The frames themselves had been painted black, so they would not be visible, and the path really would appear to hover over the planting.

Diarmuid arrived at around 4 p.m. He said he was very pleased with progress and the word went out that

Provence
comes to
Chelsea

he was taking us all for a well-deserved drink. After sorting out whatever details needed his attention, he disappeared again.

It was almost 6 p.m. when we finally downed tools. By then we had been joined by a few extra bodies: Duncan from Durham, a landscape architect who was working on contract for DG Design (Diarmuid Gavin's design company) and Clem, Hester's husband, who had come to see how it was all going.

We had tidied up the garden and, before we left, we took a long look at it. We could see what a difference the path being installed had made. Up to this, the only 'features' (apart from the ever-changing mounds of soil) were the pods. The path linked these, introduced other colours and textures into the garden and served to bring everything together. Progress!

Hester led the way to the pub, out the King's Road entrance and up and down through the very well-to-do residential areas of Chelsea, where even the cars look affluent.

Off to Chelsea with Diarmuid

On the way down the road, I decided I'd have to tell someone at home where I was off to – to have a pint with Diarmuid Gavin (I'm easily impressed). However, Mollie, whom I texted, was not! The conversation went something like this:

'Going for pint with Diarmuid.'

'Just u r the team?'

'The team unfortunately.'

'Stop txting me am in cinema with Ash.'

Due to technical shortcomings (mine), I had sent each message twice. Funnily enough, she wasn't doubly impressed with the newsflash.

I was still laughing to myself when we arrived at the pub, a typical English corner variety – typical that is of a pub in the stockbroker belt, a few of whom were inside. We missed the last few seats outside and I was just as glad. We had spent the entire day outside in the heat. Inside it was cool.

Drinks were ordered and passed around. The conversation turned to reality TV; *The Farm* had just started on Channel 5. I had flicked through it very briefly that morning (still waking ridiculously early, TV still awful). Not surprisingly, the subject of ballroom dancing came up. I hadn't seen Diarmuid's appearances on *Strictly Come Dancing*, being more of a fan of his garden designs than his fancy footwork. When asked if he enjoyed it, he was genuinely enthusiastic and was looking forward to having the time to trip the light fantastic again!

Of course the subject of his gardening programmes came up, but when Gráinne felt the need to volunteer the gem that she had never actually seen any of his gardening programmes, it was time to hail that taxi and head home.

On reaching the hotel, not wanting to break a habit, we had our *après* dig, *après* pint, pint! Then a shower, clean clothes and out for dinner. Duncan, who was as enthusiastic about rugby as he was about landscape architecture, joined us for dinner. He was impressed by the offer of a signature from Gordon D'Arcy of the Irish rugby team, who is Donal's nephew. He, in turn, impressed us with his descriptions of the gardens – and the amazing houses in them – that he was working on for Diarmuid.

Waking up the next morning – early again – I felt as if I had been in Chelsea for a lot longer than three days. Everyone at home was getting on fine without me and the girls would be back at school after the weekend – Sarah-Louise studying for her junior cert (hopefully) and Mollie in fifth class. Such a difference from when they were little and needed major organising if I was away. Now that they were old enough to look after themselves (with a bit of help from their dad) I could just leave them to it. In fact, as I'm really not the best at the whole house-cleaning and cooking scenario, I reckoned they were probably doing great and, with any luck, I would be going home to a cleaner, more organised house than the one I'd left behind.

It was to be an early start today; crack-of-dawn stuff. As tons of soil was due to arrive, there was major soil-moving and hill-forming to be carried out. So, enthusiastic as ever, off we set at 7 a.m.

Over the weekend, our site had been relatively quiet. In fact, all of the gardens had been quiet. Quite a few of them had nobody there at all over the weekend. Today though, from the moment we walked through the main gate, there was a heightened sense of urgency and activity everywhere. The queue of trucks, vans, lorries, artics, jeeps and cars was now running right down the embankment and there seemed to be no end to it. Security had increased, impossible though that seemed. We were stopped just inside the gate because we didn't have on our high-visibility vests and were grudgingly let go to the site hut to get them. We made sure to bring them home with us that night. There were more people everywhere and it was the same on our site. It felt strange to see all these extra builders, carpenters, and electricians. Many of them had been working there during the weeks before we had arrived, but, to me, it felt like they were the 'new people', not us.

The carpenters had been there on Saturday, making wooden slatted floors for the pods. These were made from a sustainable dark hardwood. The RHS insists that any wood used is sourced from sustainable resources. They are also very strict about recycling and don't allow peat to be used.

A wooden template had been cut for each pod. Because they had been individually handmade, each one was a slightly different shape and size. The floors were set on a base in the centre of each pod, stopping 2-3 feet short of the walls. This gap was to allow space for the coloured lights, which would be set under the floors, to spill out and wrap around the inside of the pods.

Today the floors and walls in the 'under-the-mound'

underground room were being laid. Each length of wood was individually measured, taken outside and cut. It seemed to us like a slow way of doing it, particularly as they knew the measurements of the buried container. We wondered why all the wood hadn't been cut off-site. Of course by this stage we were (self-professed) experts on most things and could always come up with any number of suggestions for better ways of doing things than how the 'experts' were actually doing them. As a rule, we kept our supposed improvements to ourselves. Though, on occasion, we did voice these opinions and, to be fair to Hester, George and Diarmuid, they would always listen, take the suggestions on board and either give you the logical reason why your brainwave would never work, or they would try it out. George, in particular, would always include us in any decisions and always made sure we knew what was going on. We were very much his team.

Having arrived early on Monday as requested, we started off, as ever, with shovels, spades and rakes. It was very much a case of grab whatever you find and hold onto it, as there was a limited supply of everything. For example, we had started out on the Saturday with four wheelbarrows. By Monday we were down to two, and by Tuesday we had one.

Provence comes to Chelsea

As well as Duncan, there were two more DG Design employees whom we hadn't met before: Rob and David. They very much worked as a team and were already shovelling and raking the front area of the garden. Today there was a lorry load of soil due to arrive, 30 or 40 tons worth, and we were to get the gradients and slopes right. Our job was – surprise, surprise – to shovel, wheelbarrow and rake. A giant grabber operated by the truck driver was a great help, as he could deposit mounds of soil where it was needed. Relief all round, but especially for Donal and Mark. They were the ones who, up to this, had been wheeling loaded barrows of soil over the boundary wall, up and down planks, and tipping them into place for George, Gráinne, Kathleen and myself to distribute.

Continued on p.77

The garden was to consist of a series of slopes. These started at the front at the level of the boundary wall, which was 1 foot high, rose slightly, and sloped down towards the centre of the garden, the lowest point being near the middle of the second path. It then started its ascent up to the back of the garden, almost seeming to swallow the two pods there. This was to be a dramatic sweep, rising up in total to almost ten to twelve feet. A makeshift safety rail had been set up on the right hand side, and the slope was so steep that you really had to heave yourself up by holding onto it. When you got to the top, there was a fairly large area of level ground. This was where Claire from RTÉ Radio 1 had set up her mobile satellite dish for the live broadcast that morning. There was an ISDN wire coiled around the tree behind us, and the small satellite dish was in front of us.

Off to Chelsea with Diarmuid

We were going to be on the radio. Marian was on her holidays, so we would be chatting to her replacement, Con Murphy, instead. We were all lined up and Diarmuid had even managed to put down his mobile phone briefly. He spoke in his usual easy, relaxed way, chatting comfortably, as if to friends, rather than broadcasting live to thousands. We could hear only half the conversation, as there weren't enough headphones to go around all of us. Kathleen wished her mother Happy Birthday and told the nation about her cake that had been baked in Donegal and carried over carefully for George and the rest of us to have with our cups of tea. Gráinne was completely overawed by the pods and was planning to make one for her own garden. Mark talked about how his dad wouldn't believe that he could possibly get picked to go to Chelsea, how he kept promising to get him tickets to go to the garden show instead. He was still waiting on his dad's tickets, but he had made it to Chelsea.

Time had run out by the time it got to Donal and myself, so there were no hello mums for us, just 'here's your shovel and back to work'!

Kildarton House

Marian Finucane in the garden at Kildarton with her young interviewees. *Left to right:* Ben Purcell and Charlie O'Reilly.

Left to right: Sophie O'Connell and Martha O'Flynn test the waters at the opening of the sensory garden in Kildarton.

Chelsea WEEK 1

Group One at the Chelsea Flower Show. *Left to right:* Phil Conway, Gar O'Leary, George Dunnington, Barry Murphy, Nicki Matthews and Catherine Kirwan.

The Bull Ring entrance to the Chelsea Flower Show.

The much-anticipated arrival
of Diarmuid's pods.

A view from one of the pods
as construction work
continues on the garden.

Diarmuid tries out one of the pods for size.

Catherine Kirwan with some much-needed
sustenance from the on-site canteen.

Nestled in the raised banks, the pods begin to look at home.

Chelsea WEEK 2

Group Two. *Left to right:* Mark Phelan, Gráinne Doyle, Donal D'Arcy, Kathleen Dorrian and Jackie Ball.

The newly laid path, suspended on metal trestles. The idea was for the path to appear to 'float' between the planting that would eventually surround it.

Duncan Moore from DG Design shares a well-deserved (but short!) break with George.

Diarmuid checks the lavender on its arrival from France.

Left to right: Donal D'Arcy, George Dunnington, Jackie Ball & Mark Phelan. Group Two say their goodbyes. (Gráinne Doyle and Kathleen Dorrian had left on an earlier flight).

Chelsea WEEK 3

Courtesy of Peter John Fellows

Group Three arrive in Chelsea. *Left to right:* Diarmuid Gavin, Fiachra Flannery, Valerie Duffy, Gráinne Keating, Patricia Kettle and Conor Horgan.

The first attempt at positioning the lavender around the pink, polished 'floating' path.

The team creates the 'washing-line' effect that was part of Diarmuid's design.

Positioning the lavender … again!

Additional plants wait to be positioned around the pods to complete the look.

Valerie Duffy takes a moment to view the plants she has placed around the pods.

The chill-out pod, surrounded by soft planting, looks very welcoming.

Courtesy of Peter John Fellows

The polished concrete stepping-stones leading into the garden from the reception area.

View from the underground reception of the garden.

The 'potting' pod, complete with pots and garden tools.

The garden begins to come to life as planting continues.

The completed and fully lit chill-out pod with its suspended perspex chair.

The completed communal pod, which was suffused with blue lighting and surrounded by a selection of prize-winning Medwyn's vegetables.

Courtesy of John Cullen Lighting

View from the underground
reception of the garden
at night.

The fifteen volunteers with Diarmuid, George, June and Claire: *Back row
(left to right)*: Gar O'Leary, Mark Phelan, Valerie Duffy, Kathleen Dorrian,
Fiachra Flannery, Patricia Kettle, Barry Murphy, Claire Prior, Diarmuid Gavin,
Gráinne Doyle, Jackie Ball, Conor Horgan, Nicki Matthews, Donal D'Arcy,
George Dunnington and June Dunnington. *Front row (left to right)*:
Catherine Kirwan and Gráinne Keating.

Continued from p.64

Monday really was a media kind of day; it also heralded the return of Graham, the cameraman from the BBC:

'What are you doing there, Jackie?'

'I'm shovelling soil, Graham.'

'What for?'

'This soil here needs to be over there.'

'Are you any good at the shovelling?'

'I'm certainly getting lots of practice.'

Because there were so many bodies working away in the garden, there were times when there just weren't jobs for all of us to do. At times like this, we fell back on the tried and tested 'if you don't know what to do, make a cup of tea' formula. George was usually glad of this, although it could be difficult getting him to stop working long enough to drink it. Finding mugs was something of a challenge in itself and we began to think that they had grown legs and walked. We tried to keep six hidden in a builder's bucket, but the bucket itself disappeared. After that, it was a case of searching for and cleaning as many as you could find. Gráinne and Kathleen regularly made tea for everyone on the site – including builders, electricians, painters, and carpenters – with a minimum of mugs. This worked on a rota basis: as soon as you put the mug down, the cup was reclaimed. The constant tea-making eventually took its toll on the kettle and it finally gave up with a burnt-out element. The girls were dispatched up the King's Road to replace it. It was a pity it hadn't happened sooner, as the new kettle boiled the water in half the time of its predecessor.

Provence comes to Chelsea

When and if there was a gap in the work, we would take our breakfast break somewhere between 10 a.m. and 11 a.m. The five of us, six if we could steal George away, would stroll through the Great Pavilion. As we walked through, we would notice a stillness in the air that certainly wasn't evident outside. The stands in here had barely started construction. There was very little happening apart from the odd carpenter constructing parts of displays for one or two of the bigger areas.

Breakfast consisted of coffee or tea and bacon and egg rolls all round. Not the healthiest option, but very tasty. As I've already said, returning to the site we would walk the long way back, around the Great Pavilion instead of through it, to have a look at everyone else's progress. There were a lot of plasterers in the courtyard garden section, and large panels of glass and water features were being fitted. Andy Sturgeon's site had the most amazing cubes of green oak in varying sizes waiting to be positioned in his garden. The Cancer Research garden was almost finished, planting included. A lot of the gardens had trolleys and trolleys of plants lined up around them; others were unloading theirs. Beside us, Terence Conran's Peace Garden seemed to be bringing in more and more plants, so many that I wondered where they were going to fit them all. Back at our garden, there were only the ninety box balls and a lot of soil.

Off to Chelsea with Diarmuid

In our absence, Duncan and George had been busy sculpting. Levels had been decided on for the various areas and shovels were being distributed. The grabber couldn't reach all the way over to the far side near the wall, so soil was dropped in the centre and to the right of the path. By this stage, we had covered the path in bits of cardboard, the wooden templates for the floors of the pods and anything we could find to protect it. As soon as the soil was dumped, we filled the wheelbarrows. Mark and George shared the task of bringing it around to the base of the hill at the back. The rest of us shovelled. Standing in the centre, I shovelled over the path and towards either side of the pods, trying not to hit the paths, the pods or anyone else with my spade, while also trying to avoid flying debris from my fellow-shovellers. Whoever got hold of either of the two rakes spread the soil and levelled it.

Then Hester got the call; the lavender was arriving. The truck was outside and was queuing to get in. There were two lots of lavender ordered, 800 from France and another 800 from Spain. They would only use one lot, as the varieties were different. The French consignment was the one we were waiting on now. The anticipation was huge. Along with the box, this was to be the only other type of plant being used in the garden. Would it be ready? Would it be in flower? Would it ever arrive? It was a long ten minutes.

It did arrive, and Diarmuid was there to open it. He climbed into the back of the truck and disappeared while an anxious audience waited. Eventually he appeared, lavender in hand. He was happy. It wasn't in flower, not yet anyway, although the buds were there. Unlike a lot of other gardeners who manipulate nature and have flowers from different seasons in bloom at once, Diarmuid didn't want to do this and had decided that if it was flowering, great. If not, that was fine too. It was the grass-like movement he was looking for and he was certainly going to get that. The plants were wonderful. They were, as with the box, much larger than I had anticipated and, as we unloaded them, the scent was simply wonderful. We were in France, in fields of lavender!

Provence comes to Chelsea

The unloading took a while, and it would have taken even longer without the appearance of a forklift. The forklift driver was able to lift down the trolleys and we wheeled them away. We had done some tidying up earlier, in between digging, so there was space to line them up. Each trolley had three shelves and the plants were two deep, with eight pots per shelf. Each shelf was wrapped in synthetic netting to protect the plants and they had been transported in a refrigerated truck. Mark and Donal unloaded them and Gráinne, Kathleen and myself rolled them away and parked them. Graham was there, camera at the ready. He nearly got himself knocked down once or twice by a runaway trolley of lavender. There were a few throwaway comments about lady drivers. Mark was managing the lavender as it came off the truck and, after about fifteen trolleys had been taken down, he reckoned there were 'two more rows left'. Ten trolleys later and we were 'almost there', by Mark's reckoning, anyway. Five minutes later, we were still unloading Mark's 'last three'. Donal and myself were still laughing when we did finally reach the last three. Lined up neatly were forty-three trolleys of lavender.

The next job was unwrapping. Luckily, George had a penknife – he must have been a scout in his youth. The plants were very well wrapped and there had been no stinting on the amount of netting used. A large bag of it went to the skip.

At around 3 p.m., the rain started. By then, the numbers on site had increased. Diarmuid had decided to put steps up to the top of the bank, and two metal workers had arrived and were cutting and welding pieces of steel on the path beside us to fit a bar to hold the steps in place on the bank to the right of the entrance pod. Space was limited, so by this stage the five of us had got out of everyone's way and were finding the odd job to do around the place.

I got the lavender. It was bone dry from its journey so, as it rained down on me, I watered it. All 800 pots. It was a long, slow, wet job. As I went in and out with the hose, beside me were the rows and rows of plants for Chris Beardshaw's recycled garden. This was an interesting selection of plants. The ones I particularly noticed were weeds. I know that to some a weed is only a plant in the wrong position, but these were *definitely* weeds. They were the scruffy pink flowered ones that grow out of the granite walls in my garden and then appear in my pots uninvited and spread everywhere.

Across the path were two or three people going through each pot methodically, removing dead or damaged leaves and tidying up the foliage. They had double the amount of trolleys we had, at the very least. What a job!

It rained on and I watered on.

Rain didn't stop the welders either; the sparks

continued to fly, reflecting in the puddles all around them. Duncan and George were still working on those slopes and levels. We had got the centrepiece dug down to the correct level and the front area was looking good. The bulk of the soil was in the garden, though not necessarily in the right place. The main slope up the hill, to the right of the entrance pod, needed work. We had sculpted part of this a few days earlier and had taken away some of the soil. Now this was going to have to be put back.

George laid out the lavender and box in one section of the garden. We passed in plants and he positioned them. To finally see some green in the garden was great and the two plants really worked well together. It was going to be fantastic.

The site outside the garden had seen better days. There were tools everywhere, rubbish from the builders, muck and puddles from the rain. Kathleen and Gráinne had to leave early. Mark, Donal and myself tidied up as much as we could before we left to make our way back to the hotel, wet, muddy and exhausted.

Provence comes to Chelsea

I'm surprised the taxi driver let us into his car, but thankfully he did. Once in the hotel we turned right into the bar. We really deserved this pint. It had been a long, hard day. A lot of physical work, but a fair amount of standing round looking for something to do as well. A distraction from all of this was Nano, Mark's wife, who had arrived to spend a few days in London. Introductions were made and the chat continued. The bar in Jurys Inn in Chelsea Harbour has an amazing view of the river, at least that was what Mark was pointing out to Nano. He took a lot of convincing when we told him that the 'river' behind us was actually a very realistic, giant billboard! We were still laughing about this the next morning when Donal told everyone else about it. We left damp seats and a lot of mud in the bar behind us.

That night I had my usual shower, and then decided I was still so cold that I would have a bath as well. Hotel baths are obviously now made with conservation of water in mind, rather than comfort. It's extremely hard, impossible actually, to immerse yourself completely in five inches of water.

Dinner was a subdued affair, as it had been a long day for everyone. Gráinne was feeling a bit better and had come out with us. Duncan arrived straight off the site, still in his shorts, and Nano was finally putting faces to the names she had been hearing about.

Tuesday was our last day at Chelsea. As usual, I woke up earlier than I needed to. We had decided to take our time this morning and head in for 8.30 a.m. When we arrived, there was no sign of George or Hester. They were sitting in traffic miles away, so we had our breakfast at the unusual time of...breakfast time.

This was to be the busiest and, certainly, from my point of view, the most productive and positive day we had. The builders were pretty much gone, the steps were in and there were really only gardeners remaining. Hester introduced two new volunteers, prizewinners from *Garden Life* magazine. They had their own photographer and minder from the magazine and were here to spend the day with Diarmuid working on his garden. They each got a shovel. Hester found more soil to be brought in and the digging started. Mark and myself worked with Duncan, who was finishing the main slope. We shovelled, wheelbarrowed and hauled soil in buckets up to the top of the hill to pour it back down, filling in around the new steps. Someone had organised a huge roll of bubble wrap so that the path was wrapped up properly and completely for its own protection. The area in the centre that we had dug out the day before suddenly needed to be higher. Two hours later, it needed to be lower again.

Diarmuid arrived around 10 a.m. But no, the hills and levels were not right. He explained that they were fine as they were and, yes, it would make a good garden, but what he really wanted was a dramatic sweeping hill

Off to Chelsea
with Diarmuid

and smoothly changing levels that would make it a great garden. This was the first obvious sign of stress and panic, but it came from Duncan rather than Diarmuid. If Diarmuid was annoyed that things weren't right, it certainly wasn't obvious to me. We dug on.

The two prizewinners from *Garden Life*, Tracey and Jackie, were helping to move Hester's mound of extra soil, shadowed by the magazine crew – were their arms alright? were they tired? Mark and myself, heaving a large bucket of soil between us up a hill, were wondering the same thing. After all, they had been here for almost half an hour now! Three days of digging, and I reckoned my arms were at least two inches longer than when I started.

All digging came to a welcome halt when there was a rush to get the lavender, the majority of it still in the trolleys, unpacked. This was all very well if there was somewhere to put it, but there was not a lot of available space. Half an hour later, all the plants had been unstacked, the trolleys removed and dismantled. There was lavender everywhere, up on the top bank, running the length of the garden and spilling across the front to meet the box.

Provence comes to Chelsea

Every now and then Diarmuid would disappear into one of the pods. It was the only way he could get some space. If his phone wasn't ringing, there were groups of people arriving to see the garden and to talk to him: he had to be photographed with and interviewed by *Garden Life* and their two prizewinners; kept up-to-date with everything by Hester; he had to meet a group of his horticulture students and talk to George about perfecting the rolling hills of Chelsea. He really was doing ten things at once, but his easy, relaxed manner never changed. He was friendly and polite to everyone and happy to answer any questions. What you see on TV really is what you get in real life.

Lavender was placed at various spots in the garden to gauge levels. The bags of compost, stacked high and wedged in between pots of lavender, were to be moved into the garden. We would use these to finish the slopes. They were really heavy, so the job of carrying them went to Donal, Mark and George, and some of the students pitched in also. Raking and shaping the compost was a complete joy compared to the heavy rubble-ridden soil we had been used to. In no time, the whole garden was beginning to have that much sought-after dramatic feel.

There were people everywhere and more coming and going all the time. The level of purpose and activity was sometimes chaotic, but great all the same.

At one stage, while standing in the centre area (what was to be the lowest part of the garden) the guy with the spade nearest me, one of the students, was asked to bring more soil in. I said jokingly, 'Wait a few minutes before you do that or you'll be shovelling it out as soon as you've finished shovelling it in!' Twenty minutes later, he found me to tell me I had been right. Later that afternoon, the same guy asked me how long I had been working with Diarmuid. Obviously my foresight and my expertise in soil levels had impressed him no end. He was surprised to hear that we were all volunteers, here through an Irish radio show. The Fetzer Garden team was also amazed that not only were we volunteer workers, but that we had also paid our own travel and accommodation expenses to come and work and were more than happy to do it. I think Fetzer are considering implementing the same plan next year. We have assured them that we are all available to work, and that the odd bottle of wine thrown in would be a welcome bonus!

Back at the garden, there was panic. The lavender on the bank was being watered and the water had made its way down through the layers of soil, bricks and wood sitting on top of the buried container and was now streaming merrily down the newly plastered walls onto the newly laid wooden floors inside. The container was supposed to have been waterproofed, but there was a leak somewhere. I didn't like to think about how they

Off to Chelsea with Diarmuid

were going to sort that one out. That was going to be someone else's problem.

Gráinne and Kathleen looked after teas and lunches for everyone. By this stage, we were taking the long way to the on-site canteen and back for our coffee breaks, cameras clicking away at all the gardens, discussing which were our favourites, what we would have done differently. We were by now fully qualified experts in everybody else's field (pun intended!) or garden.

Looking at the other show gardens, Diarmuid's garden was certainly the most innovative in design and his planting scheme, consisting as it did of primarily two species, box and lavender, was brave and daring. The other garden that I really loved was the one I mentioned before, Andy Sturgeon's garden for Merrill Lynch. The cubes of oak were now in place, interspersed with wonderful planting. The water feature was in, but not as yet filled. It was black, with square recesses that would become square voids when the water filled around them, repeating the square theme. I couldn't wait to see it completed. Terence Conran's Peace garden next to us sported a giant white dovecote with a grey tip. I couldn't look at it without seeing a giant missile patiently waiting to be peacefully launched, torpedo-like, into space. The courtyard gardens were magic, really small spaces cleverly designed to get the most out of them. A lot of glass, water and some great planting. Black was definitely going to be the new green.

Suddenly, it was time to go home. Kathleen and Gráinne left at around 2 p.m., as they had an earlier flight than us. There were hugs all round as addresses were exchanged. George still gets cards from last year's volunteers, which is no surprise, as it would be hard to meet a nicer, kinder, more hard-working, considerate gentleman than him.

The afternoon was bright and sunny and the three of us managed to avoid the use of all spades and shovels. I watered the lavender again. It was awkward to reach, so some of it had to be sprayed. This is not the ideal way to go, as leaves and buds could get damaged. We were still all looking closely at the lavender to see if there was any chance of it flowering in time. There were a few buds starting to show a bit of blue, but most were green. When the wind blew through it, though, the movement was wonderful, which, for me, certainly made up for any lack of colour.

The garden looked quite different from how it had looked when we arrived four days earlier. Soil had been moved backwards and forwards and up and down the length and breadth of the garden and, by slow degrees, we had finally arrived at the sweeping hills of Provence. It had taken only four days, but it felt as if we had been here for weeks.

Our departure time was 4.30 p.m. and, as it approached, we made one last trip around the Chelsea gardens. One last look into the Great Pavilion, where the real activity would start in a few days. We took photos of the garden as we were leaving it; photos of George with us, shovels in hands. We handed back our high-visibility vests and, of course, our tickets to wonderland – those precious Chelsea passes. We packed our bags and said our goodbyes. Hugs and kisses from George, Hester and Diarmuid confirmed that we had worked hard and had been appreciated. The only thing that made leaving easier was the knowledge that we would soon be back to see the finished garden and that we would get to see the Chelsea Flower Show on press day, without all the crowds. Heaven.

Off to Chelsea with Diarmuid

The hotel had very kindly given us a room to shower and change and we just had time for one last *après*-dig pint.

Donal was going home to his wife and a good game of golf in the morning (if he felt up to it and if the weather was good). Mark was heading back to hand in his notice as a chef and start a new life as a garden designer, but the day after getting home from Chelsea he would be cooking for a few hundred and looking forward to a busy weekend of weddings and dinner bookings. Kathleen would be met at the airport by her husband and two sons to make the long drive back to Donegal where she is probably still regaling her gardening group with stories from Chelsea. Gráinne was heading back to Enniskerry to construct her very own pod at the top of her garden. I was going back to Edmund, Sarah-Louise and Mollie, to bore them with my never-ending stories of Chelsea, mud, spades, pods, rolling hills, cups of tea and lavender. Lots and lots of lavender.

Provence
comes to
Chelsea

The end of the Chelsea Walk

Valerie Duffy

Valerie Duffy has had a life-long interest in gardening. She is married to Mark, an architect with his own practice in Dublin. They have three children, Philip, Megan and Ellen.

Following fourteen years of nursing in Dublin, Scotland and the US, she chose to be a stay-at-home mum. As time allowed, she became more involved in gardening and started to help friends and relatives plan and plant their gardens. Then, with a desire to better understand the science of horticulture, she studied part-time with the Dublin School of Horticulture, completing the RHS General Certificate in 2002 and the Advanced Practical Certificate in 2003. She is planning to complete further modules this autumn.

MY EARS PRICK up. A familiar voice comes on the *Marian Finucane Show* as she introduces her guest one morning in late January. Diarmuid Gavin, gardening guru, is looking for volunteers to help build his garden in Chelsea this year. 'Just ordinary people with a passion for gardening,' says he. This definitely described me and, as it happened, it also described more than a thousand other gardeners around the country. But did I have the courage to go for it? All I had to do was write a hundred words to explain why it would be important to me. Could I? Would I? Sure why not give it a go? Keep it light-hearted and humorous. It wasn't a CV he was looking for – just passion!

So I did it quickly. I stamped and posted the letter before I had time to change my mind. I didn't tell anyone. I noted the first date Diarmuid had said that successful candidates should keep free, and marked it in my diary and waited.

Some weeks later, my husband Mark sent me a confused text saying that Claire Prior from RTÉ Radio 1 had phoned – something to do with Chelsea and Diarmuid Gavin and could I attend the National Botanic Gardens in Glasnevin for a seminar on 26 February. Could I what! My spirits soared. I was into the first stage.

Of the 1,200 hopefuls whose letters Marian received, 120 were asked to attend the all-day session at the National Botanic Gardens. We were told that we would not need our working clothes for this session. The purpose was for Diarmuid to explain what would be expected of us and for him to put a face to, and get a feel for all of us. Not a name, mind you, that was not his forte!

We were breakfasted royally by the staff at the Bots and ushered into the lecture theatre where various presentations were made to us. The room was buzzing as like-minded people bantered humorously with each other about their passion for gardening.

Diarmuid told us of his first Chelsea show, as did

Off to Chelsea with Diarmuid

gold-medallist, Mary Reynolds. It transpired that both of them did it on a wing and a prayer, but look what they achieved through their determination and passion.

The full range of this passion was relayed to RTÉ Radio 1's listeners on Monday morning following the recording of the *Marian Finucane Show* on Saturday evening. Everyone had his or her own reasons for coming. Some had travelled long distances from all corners of Ireland; others had cut short their holidays to be there. Our ages ranged from late teens to seventies and older. The energy produced in that lecture theatre was electrifying and almost tangible.

During the afternoon session, we had divided into groups and each of us was given twenty minutes to design a garden. We then chose one garden from each group and nominated one person to present it. This was quite a difficult task, as we were given no specific brief and, for me at least, ideas seemed to dry up under pressure.

The End of the
Chelsea Walk

However, we all did our best and the brave presenters tried to put across the designers' themes to the audience. Names of designers and presenters were duly noted, along with the names of anyone in the audience who asked questions. This was probably a sifting-out process, although at this stage I had been virtually silent – I am more of a listener than a speaker.

The entire day was exhilarating and, for most of us, just *being* there was brilliant. We would have to wait for another few weeks to discover if we were to get any further. How this energetic group was reduced to forty-five is Diarmuid's secret and I am sure it wasn't easy. I know he took photos of each of us in our groups and took a note of our names just before we left.

My interest in gardening started at an early age: following my father around the garden doing seasonal chores. He was an old-fashioned gardener who threw nothing out. Plants were divided and relocated; electric wires were stripped and the coloured strands used for tying up plants; a creepy-crawly life-giving compost heap took pride of place near the veggie plot and was dug out yearly. I scrubbed terracotta pots for his chrysanthemums, raked leaves in the autumn, fixed sticky bands to the apple trees in spring and sprayed the roses and fruit trees regularly. I picked French beans, tomatoes, radishes, lettuce, parsley and chives for my mother in the kitchen. I was never afraid of plants or of doing the 'wrong' thing with them, because I had grown up helping out and I loved it. I became familiar with all the plant names too (their common names that is) and my father would walk me around the garden and test me on them from time to time.

So it was a natural progression for me when I had my first flat in Ranelagh to take over the garden and try to tame it. It was a modest attempt, but I enjoyed the tranquillity of it when I came home from the long hours I spent at the hospital as a student nurse.

Off to Chelsea with Diarmuid

These were the origins of my love of gardening and when the next message from Claire Prior was left for me one Friday, I was thrilled. My daughter, Megan, got the news first and delightedly told me that I was through to the next round. This was to be a working weekend. We would be making over a garden somewhere, but the destination would be secret until Diarmuid announced it on RTÉ Radio 1.

By this stage I had told a few friends what I was up to, but was still holding my cards close to my chest. If I made it through to the final fifteen, it would be a bonus.

We were told to turn up at an address in Glenageary on 9 April in working gear and to be prepared to work all day until about 5 p.m. Our brief was to make over a garden for children with special needs. It was to be a sensory garden that would encourage them to play outside.

Diarmuid briefed us and introduced us to the site project manager, Barry Cotter, and to the gentle Yorkshire plantsman, George Dunnington. All our queries were to be directed to them. We were to organise ourselves, find a task that we felt we could do, and get on with it. No organised teams, no one telling you to go here or do that. It was left entirely to each individual to know what needed to be done and to do it.

The garden was soon a cauldron of activity. Donated boxes of tools were opened, grabbed and put to work: cutting, digging, raking, clearing, wheelbarrowing, lifting, shifting, and moving. For several hours it looked completely chaotic, but slowly the old garden disappeared and a blank canvas took its place.

Diarmuid and Barry marked out the paths, the spot for the totem poles and the areas where the grass was to be de-sodded and removed. The latter was a tough job, as the grass stripper was heavy. It was backbreaking work, but Conor (who would be on my team when we got to Chelsea) hung in there until the machine eventually broke down. Then the spades came out and the remaining lawn was lifted by hand. Everyone did his or her bit.

Those whose gift was artistry tackled the totem poles. David, an artist who had worked with Diarmuid in London, guided them through the process of making shapes in plywood, cutting them with a jigsaw and then painting them. The heavy timber sleepers were washed down, lifted into a trench and cemented into position. It would be Sunday before the totem-pole appearance took shape, when the coloured ply shapes would be attached.

The snaking path was going to be tricky. Getting the levels right and setting the various textured cobbles in position was not the easiest task for a team of amateurs. Luckily, some of the team had building skills and eventually, over two days, this part of the garden also took shape.

If any one of us had been asked at this stage if we thought we could turn this garden around in such a short space of time, we probably would have answered with a resounding 'No'. But the combined energy and enthusiasm of a fantastic bunch of people, each applying themselves wholeheartedly to whichever corner they were in, meant that we did achieve it.

While some people stuck at the shed-cum-pavilion project, others worked at the old play boot (a feature of the original garden), and some opted to prepare the planting areas, digging and redigging, raking and adding compost. The front-garden gang kept the cement-mixer going and lifted out cobbles and stones onto waiting wheelbarrows, brushing and tidying as they went along. A constant chain of wheelbarrows moved in and out to the three skips, which were soon bursting to capacity. Another chain of wheelbarrows brought gravel and sand to the path areas. All of us worked with purpose, but we had good *craic* at the same time.

I think adrenaline kept most of us going until dinnertime in the local pub, but even then most of us were too tired to even talk, never mind over-indulge, so we all headed off with the knowledge that we had to work equally hard the next day.

**Off to Chelsea
with Diarmuid**

Sunday morning and once again the staff at Kildarton House welcomed us back, providing us with drinks, sandwiches, fruit and crisps. The work continued and the sun came out. In the final two hours, all the plants were moved from the front to the back garden, with George and Diarmuid placing them for a team of planters to plant. This was the part that the plants people amongst us loved, finding the correct plant for the correct place: sunny, shady, dry, poolside, a little height there, a good colour combination here, too much variegation, too many yellow tones, too much similarity of leaf texture. Everything had to be taken into account as best we could in such a short space of time.

Diarmuid was aware that many people had long distances to travel that night. Therefore, he made sure that we stopped in time for the popping of champagne corks and for a few words of thanks from all concerned. The *Marian Finucane Show* was to be broadcast in the morning from Kildarton House and there were still some small chores to finish. A small group of Dubliners volunteered to be there at 7 a.m. to finish the mulching and complete the tidy up. We had to be ready for an excited group of little people at 8.30 a.m. After all, it was their opinion that really mattered.

Diarmuid had told us that we would hear through Claire Prior whether or not we had been successful in getting through to the final fifteen. He would let us know quickly, as he understood that we would need to make plans. Somewhere along the way, I missed the fact that this process would take a week. I had heard nothing by the following Thursday and was leaving on a short trip with my daughter Ellen, so I felt that my Chelsea chance was slipping away. When I rang home on Friday and there was still no message for me, I felt sure that I was out of the running. But Megan, my other daughter (always the optimist) said, 'No, Mum, you're not out until you hear that you are out.'

Long before Diarmuid Gavin was well known, he lived – or at least worked – close to where I live in Dublin. He had designed a garden for one of the families in the local national school and, on foot of that, he was invited to come and speak at one of their parent-teacher meetings. These talks are not always that well supported, though I was there myself as my interest in gardening would never allow me to pass up such an opportunity. I can't help thinking what an enormous turnout he would get now should he make a return visit.

It was at that same national school in Rathmines that I got involved in the plant stall at the annual Christmas Fair. This is not a good time for a plant stall, but I'm not one to turn down a challenge – or is it that I have difficulty saying no? So, I took it on. That first year, eight or nine years ago, I practically lifted and divided all the plants in my garden in order to fill the stall. Most pots had nothing much to see in them at that time of year, but I did label them carefully and was able to describe each plant to interested customers. It must have

The End of the Chelsea Walk

been a reasonable success because people still say to me, 'Oh, I bought such and such from you last year.' I have been asked to do it each year since. Mind you, one woman recently asked me for some advice on trees in her garden. She pointed to one tall, mutilated conifer planted right on the boundary, 'You sold me that Val, told me it was a dwarf conifer!' It must have been an unlabelled donation to the stall.

Anyway, with the years I have become wiser. When it comes to the plant sale now, we plant up seasonal pots that fly out the door. We are really lucky to have other parents in the school who run a local nursery and allow us to use their facilities.

Another project close to my heart was planting up pots of dwarf narcissi with the sixth-class pupils of the school. I did it in when my own children were in this class and also with the local Brownie guide pack that I ran for six years. The bulbs were ready to sell in mid February, near enough to the Irish Cancer Society's Daffodil Day. We sold them at the school and donated the money to that cause. Amazingly, there were many children who had never planted bulbs before and didn't know which way up to put them or how much compost to put in the small pots. Nevertheless, it was always done with great enthusiasm, perhaps because it meant time out from regular lessons. Part of me hopes that they will remember that lesson and will continue to plant bulbs in the years to come.

The phone rang on Monday at lunchtime. It was Claire Prior. 'Can you talk?' she said. 'Of course,' said I, suddenly hollow with anxiety. Which will it be – Yes or No?

'Are you free to go to Chelsea? Good news, you have made it through.' Words to that effect were uttered over the phone. Wow and double wow. I was suddenly ten feet off the floor with excitement. I couldn't take it in. She continued on about arrangements to be made and my mind was in such a muddle that I forgot to ask who else was through.

This was unbelievable, especially as I had told some friends that I wouldn't be going to Chelsea this year because my son Philip was doing his Leaving Cert. I felt I shouldn't take time out to do it. Where did my mothering instincts fly to then when the opportunity to be part of Chelsea for five days offered itself to me? Off they went out the window! He would cope, my family would cope – I was doing this for me.

Coping is something my family is good at. I learnt that four years ago when they managed with less of a mother figure in the home while I was receiving treatment for breast cancer. Like many who have been through it, I too felt that an entire year disappeared from my life as I progressed from surgery to chemotherapy to radiation treatment with a few weeks in hospital here and there along the way. I am mindful that living in Dublin meant that I was one of the lucky cancer patients, as at least I could stay at home, and making arrangements for things like school pick-ups is so much easier. On the good days, and there were many, life could almost seem normal for the rest of the family.

One of the difficult parts of an illness like this is the long wait for results and then the wait for treatment. My diagnosis was in June, surgery followed in July and then the summer drifted on as I waited for word to start my chemo. I must confess, it did seem endless. However, my garden came to the rescue, and once again I found it to be a peaceful haven. A place to sit quietly where I could try to make sense of the numbness inside, the fear that next year I might not be here to look at my beautiful family or to hold them and watch them growing up.

In early September, a few weeks before my chemo was due to commence, I took myself off to the garden centre to buy a few Christmas presents, as I knew that nearer the time I might not feel up to it. I had so many wonderful friends and family all helping out in a myriad of ways and I wanted to thank them. So I planted up baskets of herbs and bulbs and put them by to have at

The End of the
Chelsea Walk

Christmas. I also planted up pots of bulbs for myself with the thought that, by the time their cheerful yellow heads came up, I would be over the worst of my treatment and perhaps my hair would even be beginning to grow back. That is the joy of gardening – it's all about looking forward in hope and anticipation. I was already thinking of having the energy once again to while away the time making new plans for a new garden.

One of the most thoughtful presents I received at this time was a year's subscription to *The Irish Garden* magazine. I just loved to hear the heavy thump each month as it landed on the floor through the letterbox. It brought the world of gardening right to me, and for that I was hugely grateful.

But back to the Chelsea business. We had just a few weeks to prepare ourselves for our five days away. I did, eventually, find out who else was on the team. Emails then flitted back and forth, and phone calls were made as each team tried to put faces to the names. Travel plans were discussed, as each of us was making our own arrangements and travelling out independently. My group was staying in Jurys Inn Chelsea Harbour, so we would meet up on the night of our arrival.

I was in Group Three, which pleased me no end. As I am most definitely a plants person, I knew that this stage would interest me the most. Hopefully, I would actually be allowed to plant, even though I knew that it would only be placing plants where Diarmuid or George instructed me. I understood that my role there was merely to implement the designer's plans and, much as I might like it, I was not there to be creative myself.

We were there as a team of volunteers to do any task that we might be asked to do. These tasks would not all be gardening based; some would be a lot more like good housekeeping or hard labour. There would be endless tea and coffee making, site cleaning and maintenance, sandwich runs, sweeping and washing. If we were lucky, we might get to actually plant a plant after all that!

Off to Chelsea with Diarmuid

The members of my team represented four counties of Ireland: Gráinne Keating, a primary school teacher and mum of one from Cork; Fiachra Flannery, a 19-year-old student from Kerry; Patricia Kettle, a mum of four under seven from Meath, and Conor Horgan, an ex-accountant lately turned landscape horticultural student and soon-to-be dad. My original background was nursing and midwifery, and now I could be classed as an aspiring garden designer and mum of three. So we were a mixed bag; a really good mixed bag that worked well together. But that first morning we were almost complete strangers to each other with our interest in gardening as the only common bond.

We met in the hotel lobby dressed in our super-attractive work gear and boots. At least, on that occasion, we were clean and didn't stand out too much amongst the other, more glamorous, hotel guests. The previous evening, we had decided to walk to the Bull Ring entrance of the Chelsea Hospital grounds, which had taken us about half an hour.

The End of the
Chelsea Walk

On our first morning in Chelsea, we noticed a long tailback of vans, trucks and large lorries lining the left-hand lane at the approach to the entrance. These were all waiting for permission to enter the grounds, which appeared to be very well marshalled by men dressed in high-visibility jackets. No one was allowed to enter without the appropriate pass, so we sat outside waiting for Hester to meet us. On her arrival, she took us to the ambulance gate, a short distance away. This was where pedestrians entered on this side of the grounds.

As soon as we got there, we could feel the energy of the workforce within. It was like an over-active ants' nest that had been disturbed. Everywhere we looked, there was some purposeful activity going on. Hester led us down the main avenue to Diarmuid's show-garden site. Once there, we donned high-visibility jackets. We got reacquainted with George and were introduced to the members of the Penten Construction team.

George took the time to give us a quick tour of the grounds to help us get orientated, after which we were given an appraisal of what was happening on our site and what jobs we would be expected to do. Health and safety issues were explained to us and, most importantly, we were told to enjoy ourselves.

On our walk-about, I had been surprised to note that one or two of the other gardens appeared to be almost finished, with plants in place and ornamental features intact. Our site was busy, as were the majority of sites, but it was far from complete.

There were some pods in position, nestling amongst large lavender plants and clipped box balls. Only about half of the plants were in position; the remainder was lined up on the pathway between Chris Beardshaw's site and ours. There appeared to be people everywhere: carpenters, painters and construction workers. It was extremely hectic and was to get even more so when students of Diarmuid's arrived from Kew along with a photographer.

Tasks were allocated to us, most of them very physical. The box balls were large and it took two men to lift them, so that was left mostly to Conor, Fiachra, Rob and David.

Getting the box balls in the absolute correct position was a difficult task. The site level rose towards the back and Diarmuid wanted what he described as a 'washing-line effect'. By that he meant that the level of the box showing slightly above the soft lavender stems should start at a high point, drop, and gradually rise again towards the front of the garden. The box balls were lifted, shifted and dropped again many times over before he was happy with them.

However, it was not only the height that was important. Crucial also to the design was the line of the box balls. There was a correct line lengthways, widthways and diagonally. If one was out of line, it meant that they were all wrong and the shifting had to begin again. It was not an easy task and at times it seemed to be a case of 'too many cooks'.

Keeping the unplaced plants in tip-top condition was another consideration and Patricia was soon at work with hose in hand carefully watering all the plants on site. On George's suggestion, she cleverly constructed a lance-type contraption out of a broom handle and tape. This enabled her to reach in over the lavender without having to step through the plants. A purpose-made one would have been easier, plus a hose reel and hose support to keep the hose from damaging the plants. Diarmuid, please take note for next year!

The other job for that first day was to do a big tidy-up, which involved lots of trips to the appropriate skips. All wood was going to be recycled, so it went one way. Soil would also be recycled, so it was left neatly out front and it would be picked up when the garden was complete. All other rubbish went another direction. We had only one wheelbarrow; apparently two others had mysteriously disappeared in the previous week, so we had to make do.

The End of the Chelsea Walk

Cups of tea were also high on the agenda, as Gráinne will testify to. But she must have made a good one because 'put kettle on' became George's favourite request! However, it wasn't quite like making tea in your own kitchen. It was more like a rough-and-ready campsite; a makeshift area around the back. Cups were always missing and had to be retrieved from all corners of the site. Often, if they had been returned, they would be left soaking in a builder's bucket. It was such a treat to walk up to the King's Road at lunchtime and buy a sandwich and a hot drink in clean surroundings.

Diarmuid came and went all day. How he concentrated on the job in hand, that is, the positioning of those box balls, I do not know. He seemed to spend his time with mobile phone in hand, welcoming people to the site or giving interviews. It can't have been easy. The site was exceptionally busy and, because he worked as a presenter for the BBC, there was a lot of media interest, which involved frequent interruptions.

During the late afternoon, he found time to bring us along with George for coffee. At this stage, he outlined the plans for the garden and the roles we would be asked to undertake.

I think by the end of that day we had made progress and the box balls were almost right. We finished up at a reasonable hour. Hester would not be with us tomorrow as she had other commitments, but Annette Dalton, a friend of Diarmuid's who works in Kew Gardens, would be along to help out.

Feeling really tired, we jumped in a taxi and returned to the hotel, arranging to meet later for dinner when we had scrubbed up and rested. George was now staying in our hotel, so he came with us, as did some other members of the crew, Duncan from DG Design and the two Billys, a father-and-son duo from Northumbria who brought a consignment of vegetables for Diarmuid's garden. It was a good evening with stories galore and great food served in one of the local pubs. Mind you, the non-smokers amongst us were finding it strange to be back in a smoky environment, while the smokers were delighted.

The next morning found us back in the hotel lobby in our mud-dried clothes, leaving a trail of hard, muddy debris across the carpet. It was early, so perhaps the cleaning staff had not done their job yet, but I have a feeling we were not too popular. We planned to come down in our stockinged feet the next day.

It was a dull morning, which turned worse, and there was a heavy downpour as we walked to the grounds. We were all soon soaked and this was before we had lifted a single shovel.

Gráinne and I were dispatched back up the road to do some more housekeeping. This time, we were to buy whatever equipment we felt was necessary to tidy up the pods, keep the kitchen area in order and keep the team

Off to Chelsea
with Diarmuid

fed and watered. While we were away, the others were – guess what? – lifting box balls and lavender into place.

The box looked good at this stage, so the task now was to spread the lavender out between it in as natural a way as possible. Not in straight lines and not packed so tightly together that their form could not be appreciated. Also, the lavender was to remain slightly below the level of the box.

Once again, this meant a lot of lifting and shifting with the pots of lavender being half buried in soil. Yes, you have read it correctly: ninety-nine per cent of the plants remain in their pots in all of the show gardens. And that gives rise to another challenge – how to disguise the rims of the pots. It was particularly difficult in this garden because the pots were large and because of the gradient steep towards the rear of the site. Luckily, the heads of lavender were large, although still not in flower and, by tilting the pots slightly forward, we achieved the required look. The big question was would we have enough lavender to complete the look to Diarmuid's satisfaction?

There came a time when the job seemed to be going well and the view from the elevated rear of the garden looked magical, with a gentle breeze moving the lavender like swaying grass, contrasting cleverly with the solidity of the box. But there was more to do. I was summoned by Diarmuid, given a driver's entrance pass and a high-visibility jacket, and told to make my way as quickly as possible to the Bull Ring entrance where I should look for a van with 'medical supplies' written on it. Apparently, the driver had been waiting outside with no authorisation to get into the grounds for the last hour and a half. Thankfully, we were not the victims of a medical emergency. This van contained only Chelsea-type emergency supplies, and these were plants.

I found the van easily enough, hoisted myself in and chatted to the driver as we waited to enter the grounds. He was French, I think, and not a bit perturbed by being kept waiting so long. He told me that he had a consignment of vegetables to deliver and that his contact phone numbers were not responding, hence the long wait at the gate.

When he opened the back of the van on arrival at the site, the vegetables were laid out in boxes, each plant separated by pieces of foam to prevent them falling over and getting damaged. The care that had so obviously been taken was amazing; it was as if each vegetable was as precious as bone china. Even at that, a few extra plants had been added in the remote chance that something had got damaged. I was impressed not only with the care given, but the range of colourful plants supplied. Forget your boring 'greens', think instead of blood-red ruby chard, deep purple kohlrabi, yellow, red and white peppers, purple-black aubergines, silvery purple cabbage with the most enormous leaves, onions and tomatoes, lettuce in many varieties and fluffy aromatic fennel, to name just some. These were to be planted around one of the pods, both in the ground and in large pots.

While Diarmuid decided on which he was going to use, we erected a cordon around them to offer some protection from all the passing foot traffic, hoses and wheelbarrows. And, now that they were exposed to the sun and breeze and would wilt quickly, they had to be watered carefully. Watering on all the sites was a big and important task that took up a lot of time. The plants in small pots were especially vulnerable, as they dried out so quickly. Getting the correct amount of plants ordered to avoid wastage of time and of plants must be quite difficult. Ordering too many and having them arrive on site too early increased this wastage, as was obvious on some of the sites. Our plants arrived in stages, which worked well except that in the end we could have done with a few more. I understand that the judges do not wish to see any soil between the plants. Quite a tall order on this site, because of the undulating aspect of it.

All of us worked hard at what ever task we were

Off to Chelsea with Diarmuid

given. The time just flew by; most of it, for me, spent watering the lavender and box, easing the hose along the path, and trying not to damage the vulnerable plants along its edge. As it was, I could see that we would have quite a job ahead of us in trimming off all the broken flower heads, but that would be a last-minute thing, as doubtless there would be more damaged before judging day.

We finished up at about 7 p.m., all of us filthy because of the earlier rain. Conor and Fiachra must have been really tired, but those box and lavender were nearly all in position and hopefully would pass Diarmuid's scrutiny. The site looked orderly and neat, thanks to Patricia and Gráinne. We did not intend to be downgraded this year because of a messy plot.

Gráinne was like a magnet to everyone. I think the whole of Chelsea would remember her for her *joie de vivre* – a greeting here, a kind word there. She was fantastic company and had a great way of welcoming all and sundry. No one else could have successfully persuaded helpers to lift and empty all those wheelbarrows into the skip.

The End of the Chelsea Walk

Following the death of her mum a few years ago in the hospice in Cork, she had a wish to be part of the making of a garden of remembrance: a peaceful place where patients and their relatives could spend time in quiet reflection, chatting or reading.

Diarmuid's garden had special meaning for her too because her dad used to pick lavender and put it on her mum's pillow when she was very ill. I think she gathered lots of inspiration from several of the gardens in Chelsea; in particular, the two courtyard gardens, which had been built for the use of hospice patients, and the Cancer Research garden with its optimistic, vibrant colour scheme. I feel sure that her Chelsea experience will help her when it comes to planning this special garden and that many people will find comfort in it.

Day Three for my group dawned bright enough. I

had thrown my filthy combats in the bath the night before and felt reasonably respectable in the morning in a fresh, clean pair. We were still receiving funny looks from the 'ordinary' clientele. They were probably going up the King's Road for a spot of shopping and a lazy Saturday lunch like any ordinary mortals. Not like us, the mad volunteers from Ireland! But we were still content with our Chelsea journey and looking forward to making more progress that day.

Actually, we were not the only Irish Chelsea gardeners there. Some of Diarmuid's volunteers from last year were so hooked on the whole process and still so enthusiastic about the Chelsea buzz that they were now volunteers for the other Irish entrant, Elma Fenton. Her garden was called the Moat and Castle Eco-garden, an environmentally sound and eco-friendly garden that was to contain a natural swimming pond that would be filtered organically by marginal planting. The ability to disguise a swimming pool as a natural pond appealed to me, particularly because it was going to use rainwater that ran off from her garden structure, which could, in reality, be a house roof. Potential Irish designers take note: the Irish instinct to volunteer is alive and well, so don't despair. Next year, just spread the word that you need help in plenty of time.

On our arrival each morning, the garden looked better and better. On Day Four, our jobs involved clearing the little shed at the back that Nicki's group had so carefully put together with their exceptional shed-building experience! Everyone kept their bags and all sorts of equipment in there and it fell mostly to Patricia to sort it out. Having four young children at home gave her a special talent in this area and she soon had everything transferred to the two smaller lock-ups that were to take the place of the shed. Patricia's husband had nominated her to go to Chelsea because she was rediscovering a love of gardening and developing a talent for planting up seasonal pots and troughs for friends and neighbours. He probably thought that he was giving her a break from housework! Now that the shed had gone, we hoped that the weather would stay kind to us, for we now had no place to shelter from the elements.

This was a big clean-up day for all of us. All building work was to be completed and all equipment taken away. The pathway between our site and Chris Beardshaw's was swept and washed down repeatedly. Fiachra took barrowloads of debris to the skip, along with any remaining wood. The wood-recycling truck toured the grounds daily taking the timber away. Any unused compost was to be picked up from the front of the site, so that meant more barrowing and dumping. The girls did most of the shovelling and barrow-filling, while Conor did a lot of the transporting. I imagined that we would all be several pounds lighter on our return to Ireland.

Sometime during that morning another consignment of plants arrived. These were the gentle perennials in soft colours of pinks, purples, blues and whites. Plants like the delicate upright *Aquilegia vulgaris*; the spreading foliage and small faces of *Geranium phaeum* 'Mourning widow'; spires of *Verbascum phoeniceum* 'Violetta' and *Digitalis purpurea* 'Alba'; clumps of *Centaurea montana* 'Alba' and *Papaver orientale*; the *Umbellifers pimpinella* major 'Rosea' and *Chaerophyllum hirsutum* 'Roseum'; the large-leafed spreading foliage and pink drumstick-flowered *Persicaria bistorta* 'Superba'; and, for the shady areas, there were ferns: *Asplenium scolopendrium*, lots of them, and the useful *Alchemilla mollis* and *Astrantia* major 'Claret', I think, with its rich ruby-red flower.

Larger, more structural, plants were included in this consignment: the spiky *Phormium tenax*, the rough textured *Rodgersia*, a variety of *Ligularia dentata* with rounded purplish leaves, and blue-bearded iris. The only trees included were *Acer palmatum*, but these were small and not of a very good shape.

Props and furnishings also arrived: a mixture of large patio pots for placing around the pods, smaller pots and potting-up equipment for the pod at the potting shed. Ames True Temper tools, who had donated garden tools for the making of the Kildarton House garden, also supplied tools for the display in this pod.

For the underground entrance to the garden, which in reality will be an underground car park or apartment lobby, there was a couch, tables and TV; all, I think, taken from Diarmuid's own home. The single chill-out pod was to have a dramatic, perspex seat hanging from the ceiling. A minor miracle would be needed to drill the ceiling of that pod without cracking the cement and I am glad it wasn't me with drill in hand.

Following Diarmuid's instructions, we manhandled the pots into position. Some were made of reconstituted stone. They had a smooth, rounded shape, which made them close to impossible to lift. Needless to say, these were the ones that Diarmuid couldn't get quite right and that had to be moved around the most. Finally, when they had been planted up (and therefore even heavier), he decided he didn't like them and they were lifted back over the wall for the moment. Once again, three cheers for having some strong male volunteers in the team. It was good practice for Conor and Fiachra for all the hard labour they will both will be doing when college life is over and they will be their own bosses.

I felt relieved when I was asked to do a spot more watering and could detach myself from the hard labour for a while. However, when Diarmuid specially entrusted me to water the lavender over the two rear pods, with strict instructions to be careful not to allow any water to leak into the pods, I was a little nervous. The soil around these pods was banked up steeply and there was every danger that too little water would not benefit the plants, but that too much could cause a landslide and a flood.

The options were to water from above or below. I chose the latter, as then I could see where the run off

Off to Chelsea
with Diarmuid

water was going. It started off alright, as I carefully tried to gauge how much water to risk putting in each pot, but, suddenly, as I started on the plants high up over the top of the pod, the water started to gush down behind the pod structure. In it went all over the raised timber floor. I couldn't believe it and I quickly kinked the hose and yelled for the tap to be turned off. Diarmuid was still on site, so I was able to confess. He took it in his stride and I just stopped watering in that area. In reality, I think a minor flood was a better scenario than a landslide that could have sent the soft compost down all over the path with the added possibility of the large pots of lavender tumbling down as well. Now that would have been a disaster and much more difficult to deal with.

Anyway, I wasn't fired on the spot. I was asked to work late instead, which I don't think was meant as detention. Despite the fact that I would be missing my dinner, I took it as a compliment and was delighted to be there after hours when most of the hustle and bustle had gone from the show grounds.

The End of the
Chelsea Walk

Many sites were still active, but quietly so. The floral displays were being put in place in the Great Pavilion to ensure that the flowers lasted for the duration of the exhibition, which was normally open to the public for four days. This year, it would be open for five days. I hadn't had all that much time to look around, but we did walk through the Pavilion on the way to the on-site catering trucks and it was obvious how much care was going into these incredible displays. Individual flower heads were wrapped in cotton wool to separate the heads, nail scissors and tweezers were used to pick out imperfections. The flowers were kept cooler or warmer, depending on how advanced the blossom was and what effect was wanted.

The artistry of each display was amazing. Some followed a traditional, well-tried format, like the display of *Auriculas* in uniform pots which had been placed in a stepped pyramid with a black cloth background. I believe this is how the Victorians used to display them and it is still stunning. Roses and clematis were displayed in a garden-type setting and consisted of one species of different cultivars only. Each specimen was a model of perfection. Vegetables, too, were presented as works of art and one nursery had collected ten gold medals in as many years. This was to be their last year. Transporting these specimens in tip-top condition must be a real worry for all involved, but imagine what it must be like for those coming from further afield. The exotic plants of South Africa, Barbados, Trinidad, Tobago, New Zealand and Australia all have to cope with an extraordinarily long journey and changes in humidity and temperature. The science and technology behind this journey enables them to arrive as show specimens, but it still must be nerve-racking to open the containers on arrival, wondering if it has all worked.

Anyway, back to the focus of our attention: Diarmuid's garden. George, Conor, Fiachra, Annette and me were to stay on site with the boss man himself to focus on the next stage. The lighting technicians, who were installing coloured lights into the pods, were also there, so we would be working around them a bit. Each pod had a suspended timber floor and the lights were under this so that the colour would wash up the inside of the pod, each one a different colour. It did look stunning by the end of the evening as twilight faded to darkness and the garden took on a magical aura.

We were all involved in preparing to plant or planting. In certain areas around the pods, lavender was removed, to be replaced in one area by vegetables and in others by soft, perennial plants. The lavender was then used to fill gaps in planting at the top of the raised mound where we were a little short of plants. As it was, we would not have enough to fill the space all the way to the back wall and would have to improvise with painted timber sheeting instead. The judges would not have access to this area anyway, so it just had to look effective from ground level. In many ways, the view from above was the best, which was exactly what Diarmuid was trying to achieve. It would, after all, be viewed by tenants of an apartment complex.

I ended up working closely with George. Our task was to fill the steep bank of almost 90 degrees with ground cover. We chose the fern *Asplenium scolopendrium* and the at times weed-like *Achemilla mollis*. This was a good choice for two reasons. Firstly because they would both tolerate shade and some dryness (appropriate planting is important to the judges). Secondly, on a practical level, both of these plants had substantial leafy foliage which gave good ground cover and would help to disguise the lavender pots above. We were working in a tight space. Good light was fading fast and I was trying not to lose my fingers as George made the planting holes with a long-handled, small-tined fork and I pushed each plant into position. I did remove the plants from the pots in this location as we needed to get a really dense look. The end result was pleasing, but we were going to be short of suitable plants for another steep bank at the pod outside the potting shed. That would be tomorrow's worry.

The pink-flushed polished path was revealed to us for the first time that afternoon when Patricia and Gráinne had removed the bubble-wrap protection. It looked great and was very easy to wash down with the hose and a wet sweeping brush. Apparently, last year the unsealed path was a nightmare to clean up as the dirt got ground into it, so practise makes perfect, even for well-known designers, and Diarmuid got this part right this year.

Annette, Conor and Fiachra were working elsewhere on the site, either lifting plants onto the plot or planting where Diarmuid had placed them. Once again, it was a team effort, which Diarmuid rewarded with a quick drink in the local pub just before closing time. Like the rest of us, George, who likes to have his dinner early, did not get any that night. He has incredible stamina for a

The End of the Chelsea Walk

man of his senior years. I suppose it must help to have spent his entire life as a hands-on gardener and to have never been a couch potato. One could certainly not consider him to be a man in retirement.

Sunday came; our final full working day. We had decided on an early start and met in the lobby at 7.45 a.m. (all except Fiachra, that is, who hadn't received his alarm call). The others got a taxi while I waited for him after phoning his room myself to get him up.

Fiachra was only nineteen years old – just a year older than my eldest child – but had a wealth of life experience behind him already. He was a guy with a clear vision of what he would pursue and how he would achieve it. I was the 'granny' in our group and he was the 'baby'. However, the age gap fell away between us as we both shared a common interest. Of all of us, he was the only one who expressed a strong desire to take his own garden to Chelsea in the future. He had the true enthusiasm of youth and a conviction that anything is possible if you believe in it enough. So, watch out, garden enthusiasts, for the next Diarmuid Gavin and please, Fiachra, if you want this group of volunteers to help out, do it soon before the arthritis sets in!

Off to Chelsea with Diarmuid

Fiachra and I were not too late arriving on site. This being the final day, all would have to be completed by tonight. Marian Finucane's team had arrived the night before and today all the cabling would be tested for the broadcasting of her show tomorrow morning at 9 a.m. The BBC cameras would also be in evidence, as Diarmuid would be wearing his other hat today as co-presenter of the TV show with Alan Titchmarsh.

This was a time-consuming venture that robbed us of valuable work time on site. It also created work for us, as many of the lavender plants were damaged by trailing cables, despite the care that was taken. Parts of it were fun too, for instance when Patricia was chosen to be interviewed by Alan and Diarmuid. The rest of us were put like working props in the background of the garden.

We poked and prodded at areas that had already been completed, trying to keep straight faces as Patricia had to go through several takes and still sound convincing. She did really well and I bet her four small children were delighted to see her on the television. Maybe Charlie Dimmock should mind her spot.

While Gráinne and Fiachra helped to complete the planting of lavender at the top of the site, Conor worked with Annette around the communal chill-out pod and Patricia was on her hands and knees trimming broken lavender. I was given the task of planting the 45-degree bank outside the pod that had the hanging seat. Diarmuid wanted complete ground coverage in this area. It had to cover an untidy array of long lighting cables, mask the bulky transformers, and conceal the several layers of blue plastic sheeting that came beyond the edge of the pod. It looked like a challenge.

I started by trimming away as much of the sheeting as possible. Even then it remained quite bulky as there were about four layers of it. I was going to need some substantially leafy plant to disguise it and I did not remember seeing any that would do the job well. I was allowed to choose suitable plants from the selection available and I took site suitability, leaf size, texture, height and colour of flowers into consideration.

Accessibility to this area was also difficult as I had to negotiate the rather precious, but annoying, hanging seat each time I entered the pod. It kept swinging about and bumping me on the rear end as I repeatedly squeezed by it with each plant selection. I was afraid of doing damage to it, cracking it off the inside of the pod or scratching it.

I started at the top of the planting area by scooping out soil, removing the plants from their pots and planting them closely together. My choice included tall purple *Aquilegias*, a drift of pink *Persicaria bistorta* 'Superba', tightly packed *Geranium phaeum* 'Mourning Widow', more bright blue *Aquilegias* and *Pimpinella major* 'Rosea'. At one stage, when Diarmuid checked back to see how I was doing, he thought the planting was not dense enough, although he liked the layout. So I pulled some out and started again, this time making sure that no soil was visible at all. Normally, all of these plants would be expected to put on lots of growth in their first season, especially the *Geranium* which would form big mounds and, in a real garden, would never be planted so close. The trick in getting the look right was to plant in drifts, choosing taller, leafy plants and hiding their legginess by placing larger leafed plants in front and down the slope. I came to a halt when I reached the lip of the pod. As I suspected, there were no leafy spreading plants to disguise this area to my satisfaction. Diarmuid had realised that we were short of plants and had dispatched a car to raid his own garden. I would finish it later.

Off to Chelsea
with Diarmuid

Fiachra and I were then given the task of completing the area to the front of this pod. We were to take out some more lavender and replace it with three large rosemary plants, which should step up from the level of the path. This we did successfully and then I completed the planting to the front of the rosemary around the entrance to the pod, using a mixture of *Geranium, Verbascum phoenicum* and white *Centaura montana*. With the arrival of the remaining plants, I chose white *Convolvulus cneorum* to mask the far edge of the pod. This worked really well as the silver foliage illuminated the lower edge of this planting scheme. I was happy – more than happy really – as I had been allowed to use my initiative. More importantly, it passed the grade with Diarmuid.

Pots were now also being completed. Trisha planted up lettuce in one, peppers in another and the large, silvery purple leaved cabbages were planted in another. Annette had finished the vegetable plot with cordons of tomatoes, ornamental alliums, carrots, cabbage and more lettuce. She and Conor had completed the other shady corner with *Ligularia dentata*, *Phormium tenax* and *Rodgersia*. The acers were deemed unsuitable, as were the blue-bearded irises. There were not a lot of ornamental plants left over, but there were quite a lot of vegetables that were not used. We had not managed to provide ground cover in all areas, though, as some of the less visible banks remained plantless. Had we had more ferns, *Alchemilla mollis* and perhaps some moss (for around the stepping-stones), we could have done a better job. Despite this, it really worked well.

We were working away when the glamorous ten arrived from the previous two teams. Boy did they look smart compared to us! I looked for the few faces that I recognised from the Kildarton House garden and found Kathleen Dorrian from Donegal, who had kept in touch and sent me photos, Catherine Kirwan, who was in the same group as me in the 'Bots' and Gar O'Leary, whom I remembered from all stages of the competition. It was great to see them and it must have been brilliant for them to see the completed project. In many ways, they will have got a much better understanding of the entire garden because they saw it through the earlier stages. I think this probably applies to the second group most, as they bridged that gap when the metamorphosis from mucky building site to tranquil oasis was most obvious.

The End of the
Chelsea Walk

We worked on as they went off to have a look at the rest of Chelsea. Later in the evening we would hopefully get a chance to have a meal with them and catch up with their stories. However, during our afternoon break, George told us that we would need to stay on with Annette to finish off. Annette should really be given honorary volunteer status as she kept the same long hours as the rest of us, and all for friendship. She was great to work with us and put up with the leg-pulling and banter. Thanks, Annette. You made the final stages fun, even in the dark, when you were drenched from washing down that path with minimal light.

If we had had less interruptions that last night, we might have made it back to the restaurant in time for dinner. But the lighting people were back and chased us off the site so that they could catch 'the golden half hour' as the sun went down for their lighting shots. That half hour turned into at least an hour by the time they were happy with all their takes. By then it was dark. The lavender edges still had to be trimmed in places, as each time a light had been repositioned some had been damaged. We tried, as I already mentioned, to wash down the paths for the umpteenth time and the aubergine-coloured wall which all and sundry insisted on stepping on as they entered the garden. So, no dinner for us, but thanks to Gráinne we did get a few slices of pizza. She disappeared for a while and came back with it from somewhere. Eventually we decided that we could achieve no more in the dark and finished up. Next door, the people from Chris Beardshaw's team were popping champagne corks as they celebrated the completion of their garden. They sounded like a happy crew.

Other parts of the show grounds were still illuminated and active, despite the late hour, as exhibitors put the finishing touches to their stands. The grounds had a quiet air of expectation about them. Judging would be first thing tomorrow morning and I, for one, did not think that ours was quite up to scratch yet. How it was going to get to that stage was still a mystery to us.

George had left earlier to pick up his wife Joan from the station, and would be in the restaurant along with all the others, so we decided to go directly there by taxi. Just as we sat down, Conor's phone rang. A request for Conor, Annette and me to be at the grounds tomorrow at 7 a.m. to put the finishing touches to the garden. The mystery was solved. Any one of the team would have gone had they been asked, such was their enthusiasm, but I suppose it made sense to ask us as we were most in touch with what had to be completed. The thought of

Off to Chelsea
with Diarmuid

that early rise and no breakfast again sent me home to bed quite soon after that. Besides, I was really too tired to talk to anyone!

I was not too tired to make my nightly call home to my husband Mark to see how he was coping with two teenagers, an 11-year-old, Duffy (our thoughtfully named dog) and twelve goldfish. Last night he had been revelling at a friend's dinner party. Tonight, who knows? There was a text waiting for me when I checked my phone: 'Ur in *The Tribune* 2day! Just u…in fetching rain gear and floppy hat walking across a wild garden. Am I proud or what? Mx.' That said it all.

I met Conor in the lobby the next morning, having packed up all my things ready for our departure later that day. We took a taxi to the show grounds. Everyone else was to be there at 8.30 a.m. in time for the live broadcast of the *Marian Finucane Show*, which was going on air from the garden itself at 9 a.m. That meant we had about one and a half hours before the crew would need access to the garden.

The End of the
Chelsea Walk

It was small details now that needed to be attended to. The unplanted areas were to be disguised with bark chippings. These we scooped up from the chippings that we had spread on the public area outside the garden. We knew the judges expected the public areas to be looking good too, but a few bucketfuls of bark would never be missed, especially if we took it from under the RTÉ equipment van. There was still lavender to trim, as we had missed some last night in the dark, so I shuffled around on my knees examining all of the lavender for damage. The last thing to attend to would be the path, which was still not perfect. This really was a struggle to get right, as we needed it to look good, but it also had to be safe to walk on. That would be a bit of a disaster if, after all the build-up to the show, Marian were to come a cropper on air!

Having to cope with the media attention that came as part of the 'Diarmuid Gavin package' definitely made putting the final touches to the garden much more difficult. I would have liked it to be perfect and it wasn't. This was a bit frustrating and makes me believe that what Diarmuid says about not desperately striving for a gold medal is actually true. He knows full well what is needed for gold and he doesn't give himself that opportunity.

At 8.45 a.m., the pathway was once again covered with cabling and dirty footprints. All the interviews during the show were to be done in the garden itself and these would all have to be removed, pronto, at 10 a.m., when the final group of judges would do their last assessment of the garden. Judging by two other groups had already taken place during the week and the final outcome would be as a result of collaboration between the three groups.

Marian's show was in full flight, as she interviewed the volunteers and guests, Alan Titchmarsh and Laurence Llewelyn-Bowen. I was standing near producer Ronan Kelly when a tall, smartly dressed gentleman went up to him and said that the judges needed access to the garden as soon as possible. He said that they would visit two more gardens and then come straight back. He implied that judging would take place whether the garden was ready or not. We had been led to believe that they had agreed to judge Diarmuid's garden last to allow the show to be finished. Now it seemed to me that they were just trying to make it difficult for him, and I felt like asking what difference it would make to wait until 10 a.m. Was it all just part of the power trip, a way of expressing their disapproval of all his publicity?

I told Annette what I had heard and, at the next commercial break, all the crew and equipment was rapidly removed from the garden. The third group of volunteers, my group, were due on air, so it was left to Annette, George in his finery, and some of the other volunteers, also in their finery, to get in there with the last hosing and sweeping of the path. With minutes to spare before the judges returned, the hose was dragged out, the aubergine wall brushed off and all Marian Finucane's interviewees and soundmen were standing outside the garden. After all, the show must go on.

Interviews over, garden completed, friendships made, photographs taken, it was time to check out the rest of the gardens. Our passes allowed us to remain in the grounds until 2.30 p.m., when a different colour-coded pass would be necessary. That gave us a little time to look around. Conor and I slowly did a tour of all the gardens, though I'm not sure how much either of us took in as we were both so tired. He was lucky enough to be returning on Friday with his wife Oonagh, so at least he would get another well-deserved chance to see them all again. At one point, as I stood near Diarmuid's garden, I sensed a hush come over the crowd behind me. I turned to look and saw a gap develop in the crowd immediately behind me, like the parting of the Red Sea. Princess Anne walked briskly through the gap, looking neither left nor right and casting ne'er a glimpse at Diarmuid's masterpiece, not to mention the fruits of our hard labour. Maybe she had heard that the rock band British Sea Power was due to play and they weren't to her taste.

The End of the Chelsea Walk

Unlike her, I feasted my eyes on the garden. I didn't believe it would get a gold medal, but that didn't take away from its beauty, its serenity and its changing moods in different light. It oozed a sense of calmness (without the rock 'n' roll band). I loved it and could have happily spent hours in the chill-out zone. As I left it, I felt moved and proud to have worked there. I certainly had pushed out my own boundaries, and I had done something that one year ago I would not have thought possible.

The opportunity to be there came at a difficult time for me. That journey will forever be entwined with memories of another passionate gardener. A friend who had supported me through my treatment and who would have revelled in stories of my Chelsea journey but who, unlike me, did not win her battle with breast cancer. She died in the week I wrote that first letter.

Diarmuid had indeed given fifteen people with a passion for gardening memories to cherish.

**Off to Chelsea
with Diarmuid**

The Plantsman's Story

George Dunnington

Having developed a passion for gardening at an early age, George trained as a gardener with the Harrogate Parks Department in Yorkshire. Throughout his career, he has worked as a landscape gardener for private industrial companies and as a regional landscape officer for the Central Electricity Generating Board. He was later appointed national landscape officer with National Power in the UK, and has also worked for the Royal Horticultural Society. After taking early retirement, George continued to work as a consultant for a local landscape contractor.

George met Diarmuid Gavin while they were both working on the BBC TV programme, *Gardens Through Time*. A firm friendship developed, and George has worked on several projects with Diarmuid since then.

George was born in Harrogate, North Yorkshire, where he still lives with his wife June and his mate Billy, a blue cocker spaniel who takes him for walks daily. George and June have three daughters, Jill, Carol and Sharon, and four grandchildren, Rory, Owen, Jonty and Robert.

I REMEMBER WELL the first time I met Diarmuid Gavin. It was in the spring of 2003 and I had just started working on the BBC television programme, *Gardens Through Time*, a joint venture between the BBC and the Royal Horticultural Society to celebrate the bicentenary of the RHS. This project was a new adventure for a man who was supposed to have retired but, thanks to meeting Diarmuid, there were to be more adventures ahead.

On my first day at work on the *Gardens Through Time* programme, I was planting roses in the Edwardian garden when one of the TV people brought a young man across and introduced him to me. 'This is Diarmuid Gavin, one of the presenters for this series,' she said. 'You will no doubt have seen him on TV.' My reply was 'No, I don't watch much TV. Too busy doing my own thing.' Diarmuid greeted me with a firm handshake and a cheeky smile. I was smitten!

Off to Chelsea with Diarmuid

In 2001, the Royal Horticultural Society merged with the Northern Horticultural Society. Harlow Carr Botanic Gardens in Harrogate, Yorkshire became part of the RHS as a result. The new site at Harlow Carr was the chosen location for the *Gardens Through Time* programme. The production company that had been commissioned by the BBC asked Skeltons (for whom I was working as a consultant) to supply a person to assist with the preparation of the areas for filming and to co-ordinate the delivery of plants and materials as work progressed. It was suggested that I might be interested. At the time, I had already made the decision to retire, but I realised that this was not just another landscape job, but a high-quality, high-profile job. After discussing the matter with my family, I said 'Yes.' Little did I know what I had let myself in for. The grand adventure was about to begin.

Seven gardens were to be created for the programme, each reflecting different periods in gardening over the last two centuries. The periods to be represented were the Regency period, the mid-Victorian period, the Edwardian period, the 1920s, the 1950s, the 1970s and, finally, a contemporary garden would be designed by Diarmuid Gavin.

I worked with Diarmuid on the gardens that were being made for *Gardens Through Time* and I liked the way he went about things. He had a mind of his own, as well as being a good plantsman. I saw a good example of this as we worked on the mid-Victorian garden. A fernery – a typical feature of the 1860s – was being constructed for this garden. Using the drawing provided, I prepared the area with half-rotted tree trunks and a few small rocks. Diarmuid looked at the drawing, which indicated where the ferns had to be placed, gave it back to me and proceeded to place the logs and stones where he wanted them, followed by the ferns. Certain members of the TV crew were not pleased, but filming was completed and I finished off the fernery. Today it looks as natural as you would see in a wood. A brilliant lesson – plant informally so it looks as if nature is at work.

During the Regency period, garden plants were being imported from all over the world by plant hunters, sponsored by wealthy plant collectors. The Regency garden *c*.1815 shows how people liked to show off their plants by planting them on raised beds, one specimen per bed, set in a lawned area. Another development of the period was the walled gardens with espaliered fruit growing on the walls.

Regency gardeners used lots of organic matter, such as dead animals, fish, bones, blood, urine, bird dung, night soil (human poo) and seaweed in their preparation. I remember Diarmuid making the bed with dead fish. The smell from the fish…well, I don't know how Diarmuid managed!

In the mid-Victorian era – the 1850s and 1860s – formal mass bedding displays emerged and this garden brought back memories of my early days working for the Parks Department in Harrogate, where we grew thousands of plants for bedding out both for spring and summer colour. We had great fun designing the Italian bed and marking out the design with sand. I was asked to start planting at one end. After about five takes, I was asked to slow down as there would be no plants left to plant – this is TV!

Late-Victorian gardens were often seen as status symbols. Hothouse plants and rare plants like orchids, brought in from abroad by plant finders, were housed in conservatories heated by hot-water pipes. Alpine gardens and fantasy gardens came into fashion and, in our garden, Diarmuid enjoyed constructing a feature from Sir Frank Crisp's late-Victorian garden (a copy of the Matterhorn built to scale) with the help of local stonemasons.

It was during this period that growing your own vegetables became fashionable and children were encouraged to take an interest in gardening, so we developed a small vegetable plot and a children's garden. It reminded me of the small vegetable plot I had as a child in my parents' allotment. In Victorian times, children were given a small patch of garden to sow the seeds directly into the ground; seeds of annuals that would flower quickly such as *Nigella*, *Clarkia*, *Cosmos*, *Nasturtium*, sunflowers and poppies. Pest control in this garden was the same as in my father's – soap suds plus picking off the caterpillars by hand. I enjoyed making this garden.

Our Edwardian garden, 1901–1910, consisted of a wild garden, a formal pond, old rose beds with lilies, *Nepeta* as hedging, *Bergenia* and rock plants hanging over the walls and roses on a pergola, but the main feature was the herbaceous border, created in the manner of Gertrude Jekyll, one of the most influential garden designers of the time. William Robinson, an Irishman who had a great influence on Edwardian gardeners, was critical of the Italian garden and massed bedding, preferring natural planting. I still like the Edwardian garden and find it very peaceful.

The Festival of Britain Garden was designed to celebrate the festival that took place in 1951. I remember a school trip when we travelled down to London by train and were taken around the festival hall to see the various garden features – the use of ornaments and statues, the mass annual bedding displays and the mass shrub planting, such as you see nowadays around supermarket car parks. The theme was straight lines, cubes and blocks of one colour. The floribunda rose bed was created by using a rich dark red rose called 'Paprika'. I planted 120 of these roses in a bed in the mid 1960s and it still grows.

Lots of gardeners were lost in the Second World War and those who returned, like my brother, no longer wanted to work for low wages – they felt they deserved better paid work. Building work and factory work was booming and being a gardener in a big estate no longer had an appeal. As a result, the owners of these estates had to re-think their methods and use modern machinery and other labour-saving methods. This period after the war saw a change in the attitude of the working class and they now wanted their own gardens. The RHS became a great resource, helping its members cope with the problems of managing their estates, whether large or small.

The 1970s garden was the Outdoor Room garden. At that time, the gardening style was greatly influenced by an American, Thomas Church. He lived in California's mild weather and he believed people wanted to spend more time enjoying their garden and less time maintaining it. The Outdoor Room garden was a low-maintenance garden that made use of paving, screens and ground-cover plants. Plants that thrived in a particular location were chosen and, as a result, they matured quickly.

The Contemporary garden was designed by Diarmuid Gavin. Picture, if you can, an 8-ft walled garden. Three of the walls are painted aubergine and the fourth wall is the wall of the house with a door, windows and a formal paved area. In the paved area, underplanted with herbs, is a standard *Sorbus* 'Sunshine', which produces beautiful white flowers in spring, which are followed by clusters of rich yellow berries.

Visitors enter the site through the west wall and exit to the east. When you step off the paved area, you step onto an egg-shaped lawn, framed by a black metal frame, where a standard *Catalpa Bignonioides*, the Indian Bean tree, is growing. At the far end, there is a sunken outdoor garden room, with transparent glass doors and windows.

From the lawn edge to the metal frame there is mixed planting of grasses and herbaceous plants and climbing roses and passion flowers grow on the open frames. There is a wild garden between the metal structure and the wall, and an area for the children to play in which is planted with silver birch, rhododendrons, shrubs, grasses and ferns, including tree ferns. *Ceanothus, Lonicera henryii, Solanum crispum* and *Vitus* (a golden-leaved hop) climb the wire supports attached to the wall. During the evening, the garden has a totally different feel with the fibre-optic lighting, blue strip lighting and the spotlights placed in among the plants.

One of the shots for that television programme was of Diarmuid and myself watching a giant screen showing The Chelsea Flower Show 2002. Little did I know it then but, thanks to him, I would be there in 2004 and 2005.

The gardens at Harlow Carr are now open to the public and the RHS have retained my services to maintain them and undertake various improvements. It's like magic working with the plants and with the staff, who are all keen to learn more. Watching the pleasure the general public get from the gardens, especially the older people, brings back fond memories.

Off to Chelsea
with Diarmuid

After the *Gardens Through Time* project, I was taking it easy, doing some work, watching football and pottering away at home when, in February 2004, I got a phone call from Hester, who I'd worked with on the programme, asking if I would like to help Diarmuid with the garden he was creating with the aid of some volunteers for the Chelsea Flower Show. I'd only ever been to Chelsea once and that was with my friend and colleague, Ray Skelton, some forty years earlier. Arrangements were made and off I set at 7.20 a.m. from York to London one Monday morning in May – like a schoolboy; flat cap and small suitcase.

Once in London, I got a taxi and requested Chelsea Show, Bull Ring gate. The driver, a Londoner, was very proud of his city and described the various buildings that we passed. I commented that we had two buildings that size in Harrogate and asked why everyone rushed around so much. On turning a corner there were flags everywhere. 'What's that building?' I asked. 'Buckingham Palace,' came the reply. As we drove along the side of the Thames, Diarmuid rang to ask where I was and I replied 'I'm travelling along the side of a river.' The taxi driver exclaimed, 'A river? This is the Thames!' 'They are filming at the entrance,' Diarmuid said. 'No problem,' I replied. 'I'll just pull up at the roundabout.' We did so and Diarmuid was there to greet me with the TV cameras rolling. As I got out of the taxi, I thanked the taxi driver for a pleasant journey. The look on his face. Brilliant!

I had arrived at the Chelsea Flower Show 2004 for the final week of preparation, so I only met the volunteers for the last week, but working with Shaun, Paul and Annette (a friend of Diarmuid's in a management role at Kew gardens who also assisted in Chelsea 2005), plus the TV crew who were filming the series, was very exciting and enjoyable. The site was bustling with people – electricians, builders, irrigation people and the TV crew. It was organised chaos but great fun. My wife June came down for the Tuesday of the show. The weather was good and the whole thing was a great experience. I still receive Christmas cards from the ladies from Ireland.

It was around about January 2005 when I received another call from Hester. Diarmuid wanted to know if I would care to travel to Kew Gardens for the weekend as he was working on a project. Great. I'd never been to Kew before and had only read about the gardens from books. When I arrived, BBC Wales was there with about thirty-five students. Diarmuid greeted me with that smile of his and said, 'I want you to talk about your working life in gardening.' 'All right,' I replied. 'When?' 'When you have had lunch!'

Thirty minutes later I gave a forty-five minute talk, with Diarmuid joining in. Next day, I took a tour around Kew gardens and saw the magnificent trees, the lawns, the palm house, the trial plots and the new developments in the rockery. Annette Dalton was there to give us the inside story of what it was like to work at Kew. After dinner it was goodbye and the return journey to Harrogate. I don't remember too much about the journey; just thinking about Kew gardens and the people I had met up with.

Back at home I got back into the old routine when, bang, there was yet another phone call from Hester. This time it was about a trip to the National Botanic Gardens in Dublin in February, where I would give a talk to 120 hopeful Irish gardeners who wanted to work on Diarmuid's garden for Chelsea 2005. This was a first. I'd never been to Ireland before.

I arrived at the gardens and was greeted by Hester, Diarmuid and his family. Right. What next? 'I want you to talk about *Gardens Through Time* and your Chelsea experience,' Diarmuid said. 'I'll introduce you and then it's over to you for thirty minutes.' Hester informed me that they had put a few slides together. While I stood in the corridor, Diarmuid introduced me. I arrived out to a

Off to Chelsea with Diarmuid

full lecture hall. 'Great,' I thought, 'One hundred and twenty people in a lecture theatre! Well, here goes.' Having the slides made it easier. Afterwards, I met some gardening friends of Diarmuid's, among them Mary Reynolds, a gold-medal winner at Chelsea in 2002 on her first go with her Celtic Sanctuary garden, and Paul and Edel Maher, curators of the National Botanic Gardens – dedicated people. We had a guided tour, which gave me the opportunity to walk and talk with the 120 people who wanted to go to Chelsea. All this was going on for the RTÉ Radio 1 show presented by Marian Finucane, but the producer Claire Prior still had time to make me feel at home. Talk about a military operation. And Claire can sing as well!

The 120 people were divided into groups of ten, and a small task was organised. Each person had to design a garden for Chelsea, and the best one out of the ten was presented to the gathering by another member of the group. I sat in on one group and found it inspiring. Certain people started to stand out. The presentation was done in the main lecture theatre, followed by the *Marian Finucane Show*. Marian is some lady. I enjoyed the experience.

While I was in Dublin, it was mentioned that Diarmuid had promised to make a garden for Kildarton House after the Chelsea show in 2004, but due to other commitments had been unable to start the work. Soon after my return from Dublin, I received a call to come back and help create this garden in two days from a site that had been badly neglected.

I was brought to the site in Glenageary to meet the group who were to work on the garden. The 120-plus applicants that I had met in the Botanic Gardens had been reduced to forty-five people by now. Barry Cotter, a local landscape contractor, had moved in earlier in the week and started to clear the site. When I arrived with Diarmiud and Hester, all materials and plants, turf, tools, soil, paving and ducting, were already on site.

The
Plantsman's
Story

Following a short meeting where Diarmiud explained the plan and the work to be done, it was time for action.

Considering that most of the volunteers had never really met before the seminar at Dublin's Botanic Gardens, it was brilliant to see these forty-five people working as a unit at Kildarton House. Groups were formed and the work was carried out over the weekend.

The site was cleared of overgrown shrubs, ivy and general rubbish and the waste material was put into skips. One group moved an existing shed to new location, while a small group of ladies erected a new pavilion. This was lined with boards and was open-sided so that parents could observe their children playing. Another group, working with Barry, laid block paving to create the footpaths. Pits were dug for the railway sleepers, which were then cut to size and secured with concrete mix. Flowerbeds and lawn areas were laid out.

Off to Chelsea with Diarmuid

The centrepiece of the garden was a beautiful children's cottage, provided and built by Graeme and Richard of Cosy Cottages. The cottage was decorated by Graeme's mum and surrounded by a picket fence. A fibre-glass giant boot was washed and repainted and the sleepers were decorated with painted faces, with lumber shapes added for the arms and ears.

While all this was going on, the staff in Kildarton House ensured that food and drinks were available whenever needed. By Saturday evening, most of the hard landscaping was well on its way and we all retreated to the local pub for a well-earned evening meal and drink. Everyone was excited, and certain people were starting to excel. I was making notes.

Sunday morning, back to work. It was a lovely day and BBC TV was present, taking shots of the progress for the build-up to Chelsea 2005. Claire Prior from RTÉ Radio 1 was there too – busy interviewing people as usual.

By midday, turf was laid and the borders were ready for planting. We moved all the trees and shrubs from the front to the back garden, while work on the sleepers, shed, path and water feature continued. Trees – silver birch, hornbeam, maple and crab apple – were placed and then planted, with peat-free compost added to assist establishment. By this time, Diarmuid had laid out the shrubs where he wanted them to be and certain people were selected to start planting and to assist with the laying out. All work was to end by 6 p.m., completed or not, so when it came to the last hour, tension was building. There was a site meeting and then back to work. The shed was completed, lighting completed, water feature completed, turfing completed, paths completed. Well done! What else? The shrubbery was 90 per cent complete.

Fifteen minutes left. This time was spent clearing away rubbish to the skip and doing a general clean-up. 6 p.m. That was it. There remained one box of shrubs unplanted and the bark had to be put in place. The rest was finished.

The team, especially the ones who had come from other parts of Ireland, needed to travel home, but ten people who lived in Dublin agreed to come in on Monday morning to finish the planting and spread the bark. We agreed to start again at 7 a.m. and, sure enough, everything was ready for the opening at 9 a.m.

The parents arrived with their children. The look on their faces and their excitement, I will never forget. I felt so humble and, as I have four healthy grandchildren, so grateful.

Speeches were made, the gardens were blessed, and a poem was written and read out by Suzanne Hayes, a member of the staff at St John of God Carmona Services.

My time building this garden for children with special needs made me realise again how good people can be, how they don't take things for granted and how many had given up their free time to try to improve the lives of the less fortunate. I'd like to thank them all for allowing me to be a part of the experience.

The Plantsman's Story

Gardening has been part of my life since I was a young boy. When I was about four or five years old, I would go with my father and mother to the two allotments they had, where they grew all the vegetables, potatoes, salad and fruit crops that the family needed throughout the year. There was no machinery in those days; everything was done with hand tools, some of which I still have. The only chemical that was used was the soapy water father sprayed on the vegetable for greenfly and caterpillar after Monday's washing.

I was given a small area at one end near to the garden seat where I attempted to grow radishes, carrots and other vegetables. As I grew up, my allotted area became greater until, in my teens, I was helping my parents to grow food crops and selling any surplus to the local people for pocket money. My parents had high standards in everything they grew, especially for the Harvest festival. The marrow grown on the previous year's manure heap was always huge and had to be delivered to the church on my homemade wheelbarrow. Nowadays we talk a lot about organic growing. In my youth, the word organic was never mentioned; everything was grown with what nature provided.

Off to Chelsea
with Diarmuid

During my senior school days, a kind teacher who knew I did not like woodwork or the person who taught it allowed me to spent my time working on the school garden plot instead of going to woodwork classes. This is where I was taught all about photosynthesis, the structure of plants, their likes and dislikes, as well as learning about beekeeping.

My father was a country-style butcher in our hometown of Harrogate. He would buy the animals, slaughter them and cut them up into joints, while my mother would make dripping, brawn and potted meats. I used to help in the shop, deliver orders around the town and occasionally assist my father when he slaughtered the animals.

One day my father asked me what I wanted to do when I left school and I told him that I wanted to become an apprentice with the Harrogate Parks Department. My brother, who is fourteen years older than me, had done the same thing when he had left the Royal Navy after the Second World War. My father made enquiries and I was offered an apprenticeship, which pleased my father because he did not want me to follow his line of work. He knew that the traditional role of the butcher would disappear and that I would end up as a shop assistant. He was right.

I learnt my trade in the Parks Department under the guidance of a Mr Sid Tugman and the foreman, Mr Arthur Gamble, who was very strict. These men were in their fifties and the stories they told me and the other apprentices were magic.

After three years, I was moved into the nursery as assistant to the chief propagator. Like all the old gardeners, this man had his own seed and potting mixtures and we grew *Geranium*, *Salvia* and *Lobelia* from seed.

The
Plantsman's
Story

When I reached the age of eighteen, it was time to join the army to do my national service. Up to this point, I had never been outside of Yorkshire. When I was told that I was to report to Ostwestry, I had to ask my father where it was. After sixteen weeks training, I was posted to a royal artillery base in Durham. I was not used to all the steady ways or to finishing work at 4.30 p.m. My usual working day had been from 7 a.m. to 5 p.m. and, after that, I worked in private gardens until 9 p.m., six days a week. I decided to look after the front of the administration offices, which was a good move as it excused me from jobs such as peeling potatoes! The commanding officer and the adjutant approved. I bought packets of annual seeds like candytuft, larkspur and *Cosmos*, scattered them in small areas, and then raked them in. It produced a lovely display, and it only cost a few pence.

On leaving the army, I returned to the Parks Department (in spite of being told by the army personnel officer that 'gardening is a dead-end job'!) as assistant to the chief propagator, Mr Ray Skelton. Mr Skelton was a gardener of the old school, but he had modern ideas. He had worked formerly at Water Priory, an old Victorian garden in east Yorkshire, where he had to live in the bothy even though his home was in the village. Under Ray Skelton, the standards of growing and the quality of plants reached a new level, as did the standard of cleanliness. His specialty was growing *Cyclamen* (fifty blooms on one plant) and *Begonia* 'Gloire de Lorraine'. Some of his favourite sayings were: 'Aim for 110 per cent and be happy with 90 per cent', 'Never put off until tomorrow if it requires doing today', and 'Get it done and don't hang around'. He had – and still has – a quick temper, but some forty years on I have not been at the receiving end of one of his outbursts. I was promoted to chief propogator when Mr Skelton accepted a job with a local park.

During this period, my father had died and my mother was not well. One Saturday after playing football, a friend suggested there was more to life than working all the time. 'Why don't you come down to the local club before we go to the local dance?' 'Dance? That's a joke!' I thought, but I decided to join them anyway and off to the local dance we went. Not being used to the bright lights of Harrogate, I did not know what to expect. It was different all right and I was persuaded to give it another go. Then I met this young lady in a blue dress, and we had a cup of tea and talked. Some forty-two years on, we have three daughters and four grandchildren. Mother didn't live to see the wedding, she was happy with the lady in the blue dress.

At this time the local parks were being modernised. I was not appointed nursery manager and I felt let down as I was already doing the job. Then along came Ray Skelton again who had been appointed garden

Off to Chelsea
with Diarmuid

superintendent in a big complex with an old house, Victorian gardens and greenhouses. He wanted someone in the greenhouses and grounds and, as I needed a change and thought I would like to go into the commercial side of gardening, I accepted the post.

Some years later, I became head gardener at Beckwith Knowle, a large, run-down estate with extensive gardens in Harrogate. My job was to restore the gardens, which had been neglected. In one of the grassed areas, there was an old croquet lawn that was full of weed and dead grass. The first task was scarify the area, after which we fed and mowed the grass on a regular basis until the croquet lawn was restored to its former glory.

The next challenge was to build a cricket ground in the field next to the main gardens. This we did in autumn and we had great fun using this facility. As a sideline, I used the rest of the field to keep 240 laying hens as well as geese and turkeys for Christmas and Easter.

One of my jobs was to assist the chemist with field trials in the use of pesticides and herbicides. I found this work interesting and challenging. To this day, I still believe there is a place for such products, provided they are applied by experienced operators who use the correct chemical for a specific problem.

This period, from 1963 to 1972, was a very happy time for me, my wife June and our three daughters Jill, Carol and Sharon. Unfortunately, the site was closed, but I was asked to stay on until it was sold. During the winter of 1972, the Central Electricity Generating Board bought the site to develop the area as its headquarters for the north of England. I joined them in 1973.

As the person supervising labour on the redevelopment, I was asked to attend a site meeting with the young landscape architect who was designing the new layout. When I saw the plans for the site I was shocked. Right in the area where the treasured croquet lawn lay, a glass-faced building with a swimming pool in the basement was to be built.

I was asked for my opinion and I told them that I did not like what was proposed. There had not been sufficient thought given to moving young trees and the type of shrubs that were to be used were wrong for the area. The site is on the edge of the countryside and I proposed moving trees and shrubs to the redeveloped area around the offices and the new car park. I would select trees and shrubs that are native to the area such as oak, ash, rowan, thorn, wild rose, hazel and honeysuckle. The site required 15,000 shrubs and I promised the committee that by propagating shrubs from the stocks on site, I would have the plants ready by the time the building was completed. The problem with propagating this amount of shrubs was where to store them. With the agreement of the contractor who was building the new complex, we were able to landscape parts of the site while construction work was going on. This meant that by the time the buildings were ready for use, 95 per cent of the site would already be landscaped and looking very mature. My proposals were approved by the company and by the local authority.

At this point I was asked to visit the Birmingham area where they had a regional landscape team servicing the power stations across the Midlands. On returning, I made all my recommendations. A position of landscape officer for the North of England power stations was created and I was asked to apply. I did and was successful.

I worked alongside one of the research officers. One of the suggestions was to re-use the waste heat from the water before it was cooled through the cooling towers and returned to the nearby rivers. After some trial and error, we were able to grow tomatoes hydroponically (in water) from April to December. We also grew cucumbers and peppers. The end result of these

Off to Chelsea
with Diarmuid

experiments is that at Drax Power Station, the largest coal-fired power station in the UK, they have a 20-acre greenhouse growing the crops very successfully. This is something I am proud to have been a part of. I had two wonderful years working on this project.

I also worked on other projects during this time: landscaping, and later maintaining, the site, planting trees (not just on-site but in the surrounding villages) and building an 18-hole golf course, a bowling green, football pitches, cricket pitches and tennis courts to be used by both staff and the general public. We also planted trees, shrubs and wildflower meadows on the ash mounds known as PFA – pulverised fuel ash.

I was encouraged by management to get involved with local villages by supporting their annual shows and flower festivals, giving slide shows and talks to various committees and groups, including schools. I had good times meeting all the people and talking to the different age groups.

Unfortunately, the UK government decided to privatise the industry and the landscape team was disbanded. It was sad for me to watch people I had employed, in the belief that their jobs were secure, being made redundant. I was asked to join National Power as landscape officer for the area of England and Wales.

The work was hard and frustrating at times, but I enjoyed travelling around the beautiful countryside. My first task was to eradicate Japanese knotweed, which was out of control in the south of Wales, but I had other, more pleasant projects as well. Among them was helping volunteers to preserve wetlands on the banks of the Thames, developing an environmental centre for schools by turning a disused quarry into a nature reserve for water birds, and building a garden for the disabled and blind, using shrubs that had scented foliage or flower.

However, the hard work eventually took its toll. I seemed always to be dashing – with files and plans and overnight bag – from the south coast of England to the north, and my health suffered and I had a spell in hospital. A visit from my manager with the brown envelope told me it was time to go and I retired, fifty-nine years young.

One of my greatest pleasures was the local football club, Harrogate town AFC, where I had played after leaving school and after my time in the army. Once I was married and had a family to support, I stopped playing. Years went by and then one day I was asked if I would have a look at the pitch. When I arrived at the grounds the place was a tip. Facilities were poor, the playing surface a bog, drains were blocked – the club was ready to fold. I helped the new committee to drain the pitch and improve the facilities and, after two years, I became chairman of the club. We developed a youth football programme and progressed through the leagues. I have retired as chairman, but still look after the pitch with my brother and friends. The league honoured me with a long service award and I hold the position of life president and enjoy seeing my grandchildren, Rory and Owen, playing for the local junior side.

Off to Chelsea
with Diarmuid

After my retirement,I worked on a consultancy basis, again with Mr Ray Skelton, pricing work, dealing with quality control and working on various projects. I was also busy in my spare time babysitting three of our grandchildren with my wife June. I did not want to miss out on this as, in my younger days, it seemed to me that I had been away a lot working, although my daughters still talk about the times when I raised hens, geese and turkeys.

February 2005. After the opening of the garden at Kildarton House, myself and Diarmuid returned to have a bite and discuss who the fifteen people would be who would go to Chelsea. How do you choose fifteen people for Chelsea? To be fair, you could have given that list of forty-five people to anybody to pick out fifteen and not one of them would have let you down, they were all so good.

As Chelsea time drew nearer, Hester and I exchanged calls and discussed the Chelsea show and the plan of attack: plants to be ordered, the building contract to be put in place. While all this was happening, Diarmuid would be busy with other projects.

It was arranged that I should travel down from Harrogate on the Sunday two weeks before the show to stay with Hester and her husband, Clem. Monday morning, 9 May, arrived, and I was on site at 7.30 a.m. to meet with the builders, who had made a start, digging footings and building walls, putting in place the container which eventually would be covered with soil and used as a reception and entrance to the gardens.

On that same Monday, the first group of volunteers arrived from Ireland. Phil Conway, Gar O'Leary, Barry Murphy, Catherine Kirwan and Nicki Matthews. After the site induction by Ranjith, the managing director of the building contractors, we all went for a walk around the Chelsea site, stopping off at the canteen for a talk, a bacon sandwich or whatever took our fancy. On the walk around, we saw everybody beavering away – building walls, planting mature trees, making ponds – then I heard this voice say 'Hello, George.' There, working on Elma Fenton's show garden (another Irish entrant) were three of the ladies I worked with last year on Diarmuid's garden. I introduced them to this year's group. Brilliant.

On returning to the site, I explained the jobs in hand to the group. First, clean up the site, and, most important, establish a corner to the rear for making a pot of tea.

Nicki, having worked in the building industry, knew all about levels, so she assisted Matt, a South African now settled in England, to prepare the site levels for when the pods arrived. Lots of earth was moved, building blocks were moved to assist the builders, and concrete was mixed. Mick, the site foreman, another Irishman, was a good man. Will, the digger driver, and all the construction team were willing to make the work easier. Barry, a young student, exclaimed 'I have learned more about landscape work in these four days than in the two years at college.' Phil had a lovely sense of humour and was good with a shovel (he should have had a JCB!) but, like the rest of us, he loved the experience of being at Chelsea. The two ladies, Catherine and Nicki, were not afraid to lift blocks and move earth, and they made good cups of tea and sorted out my mobile phone for me.

For dinner, it was a steady walk through to the King's Road for lovely healthy sandwiches. On one occasion, I passed the time of day with a Chelsea pensioner, ninety-something years young, dressed in his crimson uniform and dark blue hat. I thought of my own father who had fought in the First World War and had a chestful of medals. We should be proud that they have such a place to retire to. It was through them that we have the life we lead today.

Off to Chelsea with Diarmuid

When Claire arrived on site to do a live interview with Diarmuid, everyone was excited. Sadly, the volunteers had to go home on Thursday after their four days in Chelsea, but they all looked forward to their return on Sunday, 22 May before the show opened. On Friday, we had no volunteers, but two of Diarmuid's friends, Rob and David (fellow-Yorkshiremen now living in London) came on site to help.

Small problems do crop up – they are there to be overcome – like will the roof of the container support the weight of the soil? Ranjith, with his usual thoroughness, decided to strengthen it with girders – better to be safe than sorry. By this time, the black granite tiles were being placed on the 8-ft wall, the bases were in place for the pods and the interior of the container was being lined.

On Saturday, 14 May, the second set of volunteers – Mark Phelan, Donal D'Arcy, Jackie Ball, Gráinne Doyle and Kathleen Dorrian – arrived on site. The usual induction and tour of the site took place. There was not a lot happening in the Great Pavilion except for joiners erecting timber stands to be ready for the arrival of the exhibitors. Outside, in the show gardens around the perimeter, everyone was beavering away – two young men were thatching the roof of the Chelsea Inn and a huge crane was lifting giant sheets of glass for one of the displays.

On our site, the low walls down the side of site were being built and the pods arrived, gleaming white, with a giant grabber to lift them into place. The canteen was upgraded and Kathleen unwrapped a beautiful cake she had made. There were sweets too.

The builders were well advanced by now and, in my own mind, I thought that 95 per cent of the work would need to be completed by Saturday, 21 May. Diarmuid was busy with the BBC, dashing in, checking, instructing. Hester likewise. When will the plants arrive? Any problems?

We helped the builders cover the roof of the container with soil, placing blocks to the front to save on soil and avoid slippage. The weather was mixed, but not enough to stop work. The routine was to get up at 5.45 a.m., start work at 8.30 a.m., finish between 7 and 8 p.m., drive home discussing the day's work, shower, have a meal and then to bed. At 5.45 a.m., up again.

The pods were now in place and we decided to cover them with plastic to avoid damage. We started to shape the area and prepare foundations for the path. At 6 p.m., the builders asked us if we would fill in the spaces between the blocks with concrete. There was no moaning, we just got it done. I mixed the concrete and Donal organised the pointing, with the team and Hester assisting. The lady never gets tired!

On Sunday, 15 May, Marshalls arrived to put in place the raised path: exterior ply sitting on top of metal stands. When they had finished, the path looked like glazed marble. Beautiful.

While all this was going on, the site had to be kept tidy: all rubbish brought to the skip, timber separated for recycling, covers placed for protection on the newly completed path. When the electricians arrived to wire the pods, we helped to lay cables and mark out where they were. We were OK, up to date.

Hester informed us that the box balls were to arrive on-site. They arrived on Monday, followed by the lavender – all on double-decker trolleys. The first job was to give them a good watering. The lavender plants were full of root and were of good quality.

Then the 300 bags of compost arrived on pallets and they had to be loaded into place by hand. At Diarmuid's request, I laid out a sample of box and lavender to get a feel for what the planting would look like. I think he approved. I also laid out a line of lavender to create the shape that had been planned, but this wasn't right. Discussions followed and Diarmuid said, 'You know, like a washing line dipping in the middle.' I got the idea. We were on our way. More earth moving, more taken out of the middle, more added on the slope, level left to right – and there we have it, a washing-line effect from front to back. Diarmuid had another look, smiled, and nodded to show he was happy.

By this time, most of the building material had gone off-site, so we had room to unload the plants. The *Lavendula Augustifolia* was in 12-inch pots. They were heavy but we managed, one pot per person. The ninety box balls were well watered and heavy. It took two people per plant to lift them. The planting worked out at fifteen per row, with about two metres between the rows. There were straight lines whichever way you looked. Rob and David loved this part; they both had a good eye for levels. We were joined by Duncan Moore from DG Design, another of Diarmuid's friends.

We planted all the box balls in their pots. Once that was sorted, we started on the lavender. The night before, after we had all gone home, Diarmuid had made a start at the front, planting the lavender, averaging five plants per two metres. We continued the next day but, unfortunately, the team had gone home. This left Rob, David, Duncan and myself with Diarmuid and, when available, Hester, who was busy checking things with the builders. Diarmuid was not happy with the box. It was too low, hidden by the lavender. We made adjustments and Diarmuid approved.

The last group arrived on Thursday, 19 May and were given the usual induction tour of the site, a cup of tea and a chat. The Chelsea garden site this group saw when they arrived was completely different from the one the two earlier groups had seen. In most of the outdoor gardens, as in our own, the building works were nearly complete, and lots of wildflowers and herbaceous plants were arriving. In the pavilion, groups were starting to arrive. I felt sorry for the Caribbean and Jamaican exhibitors with all their exotic plants because the nights were bitter cold and they had to cover their plants with matting to protect them. The Chelsea Pensioners' display, which featured lots of poppies, needed grow lamps to give extra light to bring the blooms out in time for the judging. This is the usual practice in nursery growing. Nothing is too much trouble to achieve perfection.

The last group was made up of Fiachra Flannery, Conor Horgan, Gráinne Keating, Patricia Kettle and Valerie Duffy. By this time, most of the low part of the garden was planted. I shared the watering with Valerie Duffy, who was always smiling. When we were making the garden in Dublin, I didn't notice Valerie until we started to plant the shrubs. When I saw her at work, that's when I knew Val had to go to Chelsea.

The
Plantsman's
Story

The rest of the box and lavender were moved to the top of the covered container, now referred to as 'reception'. This was hard physical labour, but there were no complaints from anyone.

Diarmuid went shopping for more plants to be used around the pods – herbaceous plants, exotic plants, and, best of all, prize-winning vegetables supplied by Mr Medwyn Williams, winner of ten Chelsea gold medals. All the vegetables were individually grown for pots: tomatoes, lettuce, beet, kale and many more.

Each of the six pods had a function: one served as an entrance to the reception; one as an entrance from reception to the garden; one was as a potting shed that contained garden tools brought all the way from Ireland; one was an office with a table and seat; one was a communal area, with seating for relaxing, and the final 'chill-out' pod – the only pod which was open on two sides – had a perspex seat hanging from the ceiling. All were fitted with timber floors and the lighting for each was a different colour. The extra plants were to be used around four of the pods: the vegetables around one; exotics around another; herbaceous around the third and, around the potting shed, foxgloves, ferns, evergreens and herbaceous. It was Friday, 20 May, and things were coming together.

But we had to push on. On Saturday we were joined by Annette and, apart from Matt, the builders were all gone. We put in place the finishing touches and put up notices for the front and side explaining what the garden was all about. The painters were finishing off the low wall in aubergine, Gráinne and Patricia were clearing out the pods. Never a dull moment but no panic. Diarmuid had a final look at the pods, at the hill, and at all the herbaceous plants. Then he went on to his other work with BBC.

Hester and Clem left on Friday to go to Italy for a short break and I moved into the hotel where the team were staying. We were joined by Mark, a quiet, true professional who works with Diarmuid overseeing various projects. One of the remaining tasks was to take the rubbish to a nearby skip. This was done by Gráinne, a bubbly schoolteacher. I asked if she needed help; she didn't. The lady used her charm to get the Australians working near the skip to unload for her. As they say in England, Gráinne 'could sell coal to a coalminer'. Val worked happily with the flower displays. Fiachra, a quiet lad and very knowledgeable for his years, worked with Conor, both of them busy with the jobs in hand. We worked late on Saturday night using the garden lights to see where we were planting.

Sunday arrived and 90 per cent of the work was finished. Now for the part that wins medals, the final touch. I sensed Diarmuid was anxious, but I knew he was pleased. The lavender was not going to flower, but then, who said it would? When the wind blew, the lavender moved like grasses in a meadow. There were flashes of colour around each pod and we planted pots to stand on the path, but this made the garden look cluttered. Diarmuid removed them and used the plants elsewhere. The builders arrived to remove the rest of the materials from the site, the last touches were given to the paintwork and David, who had painted the Disney-like characters on the sleepers in Kildarton House, was back again painting a mural of a Swiss cheese plant, a *Monstera*, in reception. While all this work was going on, a TV crew drifted in and out taking pictures and talking to the team.

The Plantsman's Story

Mid-morning on Sunday, 22 May, the RHS arrived with the bark mulch to be spread from our stand to the path edges. This they do around all the sites. The paths were washed to remove stains or damaged flowers, lavender spikes were removed and the rest of the rubbish was brought to the tip.

Visitors started to arrive at the stand. First to arrive was a Chelsea Pensioner and, as I showed him in, I thought he was about to slip and I got hold of him. 'No problem, just an old war wound in my right hip,' he said. I wish I could have spent more time with him. He would have had some right tales to tell.

Then, just as Diarmuid got hold of a brush, Alan Titchmarsh arrived with his crew for an interview. Myself, I was 98 per cent (not 100 per cent) happy, but no more could be done. All the plants had been used and there was just a handful of vegetables left. These extra vegetables had been grown organically by one of Diarmuid's students from another project. During the course of the project, eight students came in two batches to assist and, hopefully, as well as improving their horticultural knowledge, they learned a bit about working as a team. As well as the students, we had two ladies who had won a competition in *Garden Life* magazine and part of the prize was a day working on Diarmuid's stand (they got handed shovels as well!). I'm sure they enjoyed the experience.

Off to Chelsea
with Diarmuid

By mid afternoon, the whole volunteer team arrived back to prepare for Monday morning's live broadcast of the *Marian Finucane Show*. I am sure the first and second groups were pleased to see the final result. There was a lot of banter about who had done the most, which was lovely to listen to.

Now I had time to go for a walk in the main hall to look at the magnificent displays, the best displays for this time of the year. Everybody was still working away and they all deserved credit for the effort they had put in. Throughout my time in Chelsea, the friendliness and willingness of people to share tools, wheelbarrows, hose pipes and, if asked, tips is always heartwarming.

My number two daughter, Carol, paid us a surprise visit and I introduced her to the team. Then we went for a walk around the site, camera clicking away. The colours on the displays were brilliant: *Begonia* with blooms 150mm across, *Delphinium* with 4-ft stems, bursting with blooms, roses with beautiful scents, a clover specially brought into bloom for this week, orchids out, carpet-bedding displays, you name it – they were all there at Chelsea. By 5 p.m., it was time to say cheerio. It had been a lovely surprise and the photos turned out brilliant. They're now in my 'Chelsea Experience' album.

After saying goodbye to Carol, it was time to go to King's Cross Station to collect June who had travelled down on her own. In forty-three years of marriage I had never been away on my own for two weeks and it was great to see her. We joined the team who were enjoying a meal and they all made June feel very welcome. The company was great.

Monday, 23 May, and judging day had arrived. Conor, Valerie and Annette started early checking around, washing paths and giving a final polish to the garden. Hester arrived back from her trip and was delighted with what she saw. She was especially pleased to hear that all the plant material had been used. At 8 a.m., everybody was ready for the interviews with Marian, including Diarmuid and myself. As usual, Claire was organising everybody behind the scenes. There was one small hiccup during an interview when the radio crew dragged wire over the corners and damaged the lavender. It was not a real problem and was quickly sorted out. Then we were informed that the judges were about to appear, so we moved quickly away from the display and completed the interview outside the boundary.

To help the judging process, every designer who exhibits a show garden in Chelsea must state his or her aims so that the judges know what the designer wants to achieve. Diarmuid's entry was described as 'a garden surrounded by flats where the people could get together. It would have concrete pots and outdoor rooms surrounded by small allotments to encourage them to get outside to work or play. Visitors enter from an underground car park or from the foyer and emerge into an undulating ramp, like a ski-jump, planted with box and lavender. The two concrete C-shaped paths act as catwalks suspended above the planting. The pods create sculptural interest and the whole garden is reflected in the polished black stone wall. The planting is simple; box and lavender with small plots around the pods.' While the garden is being built, the stewards visit the site to see if things are being done to plan. These notes are passed to the judges, who then make the decision. Everything is run like a military operation.

The judging over, we breathed a sigh of relief and had time for a stroll around the site. All the works around the perimeter were finished but, within the Great Pavilion, everybody was still beavering away. By this time, I had got to know a few of the exhibitors and, even though they were busy, they were quite happy to pass the time of day.

By midday, the team of volunteers were ready to head home to Ireland. Goodbyes were said and hugs and kisses exchanged. We were happy and sad at the same time. June and I walked around the site when everybody had gone. By now, everywhere was spick and span in readiness for the visit from the royals, which would take place from 3 p.m.

During an earlier conversation, Diarmuid had said that June and I were the two people he wanted to represent him on his stand during the royal visit, so we took our places there. I had even had my suit cleaned for the occasion – I only wear it for births, weddings and deaths – and June looked lovely.

First to arrive was the Duke of Kent, then everybody else except the Queen, who was away, we were told, in Canada. June recognised other celebrities, Gloria Hunniford among them. A rose grower had named a rose after her daughter, Caron Keating. A nice thought.

In the pavilion overlooking our display, unknown to me, Diarmuid was keeping a beady eye on things. Brilliant! Professional to the end.

Off to Chelsea
with Diarmuid

By now, evening was approaching and it was turning cold. Where were my overalls? We had a walk around, then returned to the hotel, but without the others it felt like a bit of an anti-climax. We went out to the pub on the corner for our evening meal, which included sticky toffee pudding, and then it was early to bed.

We spent Tuesday at the show with two friends from Yorkshire and the weather was fine. In previous years, the show ended on the Friday. This year it was extended to Saturday, and the extra day meant the place was less crowded, which allowed better viewing. We visited Diarmuid's garden and discovered that we had won a silver-gilt medal. This, I thought, was fair. They don't give golds away that easily. The other displays around only got bronze. The Chelsea Pensioners' display won a gold medal and also Best In Show. It had a thatched inn with real ale, a vegetable plot and woodland scene, including poppies. I thought the awards it got were well deserved.

I felt privileged to have been asked by Diarmuid to be part of the team and to work with and enjoy the company of so many wonderful people. Like the previous year at Chelsea, the memories will remain with June and myself forever.

It was time to go and to say our goodbyes, first to Hester – a lovely person and a true friend – and then to Diarmuid. A firm handshake, a smile, a thank you and off we went. Will the fairytale continue?

The Hanover Quay Garden
Plant List

Designed by Diarmuid Gavin
Chelsea Flower Show 2005

Achillea grandifolia
Alchemilla mollis
Allium aflatunense
Aquilegia 'Crista Barlow'
Aquilegia 'Hensol Harebell'
Aquilegia vulgaris 'William Guinness'
Anthriscus sylvestris 'Ravenswing'
Asplenium scolopendrium
Astrantia major 'Roma'
Buxus sempervirens
Dryopteris filix-mas
Erodium manescaui
Geranium phaeum 'Samobor'
Geranium phaeum 'Alec's Pink'
Geranium sylvaticum 'Mayflower'
Geranium masculatum 'Elizabeth Anne'
Lavandula angustifolia
Ligularia 'Britt-Marie Crawford'
Papaver orientale 'Patty's Plum'
Persicaria
Phormium 'Sundowner'

Pimpinella major 'Rosea'
Polemonium 'Lambrook Mauve'
Potentilla 'White Caveen'
Rodgersia 'Brunlaub'
Rosmarinus officinalis
Thalictrum aquilegifolium 'Thundercloud'
Thymus
Verbascum 'June Johnson'
Verbascum phoeniceum 'Violetta'

VEGETABLES

Aubergine 'Neon'
Cabbage 'Autoro'
Lettuce 'Frisby'
Ruby Chard
Tomato 'Floridity'
Tomato 'Myriad'